SATAN UNMASKED

A SPIRITUAL AND THEOLOGICAL EVOLUTION OF SATAN

BOOK ONE

By Tekoa Manning

www.manningthegatepublishing.com

Also, By Tekoa Manning

Walter: The Homeless Man: a novel

Polishing Jade: a novel

Thirsting for Water: a devotional

Jumping for Joy in the Midst of Sorrow: a devotional

The Spirit of Leviathan, Jezebel, and Athaliah: a teaching book on spiritual warfare.

Unmasking the Unseen Series:

Satan Unmasked: Book One

Spirits Unveiled: Book Two

Wolves Unseen: Book Three

King Revealed: Book Four

ISBN: 978-1-7374020-2-2 (Manning the Gate Publishing LLC)

Satan Unmasked: Book One Copyright © 2023 by Tekoa Manning
Unmasking the Unseen Series

Editor – Jo Fouts Zausch

Book Cover by Lynette Marie Smith
Graphic Design & Marketing

Picture on Cover by CoreRock

Contents

INTRODUCTION...

Chapter 1 ....

SATAN IN THE OLD TESTAMENT.................. 1

Chapter 2...

A BODY DIVIDED 11

Chapter 3...

THE SERPENT 25

Chapter 4...

PRINCIPALITIES AND POWERS...................39

Chapter 5...

WHO IS SATAN? 47

Chapter 6...

THE SATAN IN THE MIRROR 55

Chapter 7...

THE LITTLE GODS PART 1 63

THE LITTLE GODS PART 2.........................75

Chapter 8...

THE EVIL INCLINATION 95

Chapter 9...

THE KING OF TYRE................................. 105

Chapter 10 ....

CAN ANGELS SIN? 125

Chapter 11..

SATAN IN THE NEW TESTAMENT............145

CLOSING 181

Introduction

As a young girl I was always interested in the occult. Many times those gifted in the prophetic are. Tarot cards and Ouija boards were forbidden in my home growing up. Our home was more *Leave it to Beaver* or *Father Knows Best* unless one of my mother's brothers came to our house for a duration in order to detox and get right with the Lord. Growing up, I was raised in an Assembly of God, charismatic "church." We went to the building every time the doors were open. Once when I was in middle school or my first year of high school, the church had a 21-day "revival," and we went each night. Homework involved watching the spectacle of women getting a touch of the Spirit and running laps around the outside perimeter of the sanctuary. Hands floundering about and men and women shouting Hallelujah. It almost makes me sad that the Body of Messiah lacks the excitement I once witnessed as a youth. However, many believers have gained knowledge along the way, even discerning what emotionalism is versus the real thing.

Instead of homework or studying, my siblings and I were focused on men and women who came to speak at the congregation. These larger-than-life prophetic evangelists would walk up and down the aisles until their eyes would rest on one specific person. The evangelist would mosey over, ask them to stand up, request their name, and then proceed with "I hear the

Lord say or thus sayeth the Lord." It looked and sounded something like this:

Speaker: "Are you enjoying this? God is good, isn't He? God is good all the time! Now, Sister, who do you have here with you? Is this your mother? Yes, yes, well, I just walked by, and I heard the Holy Spirit say, "tell her, her pain is ending. Sister, you've been in pain a very long time. And not just physical suffering, but you've been hurt by someone who you truly honored. But tonight, I hear the Father saying, "Rise up, daughter of the highest!" Women and men would raise their hands up, shaking them around. Shouting praises to the Lord. Tears the size of Texas would run down their cheeks. My young brain would think, "How do they know all these things? Were they truly hearing from God?"

Soon, I was old enough to make friends and spend the night at a sleepover. I learned that my friend's mother bought a Ouija board. One night we began to take it out of the box and look at it. I was raised that this was witchcraft and not to dabble with such things, but my young 12-year-old mind was curious. I recalled the church evangelist who seemed to bring words of affirmation or exhortations and rebuking shouts at Satan. They told the enemy he better flee, but now my friends were telling me that a board could predict my future. My young mind spun out of control. "Could I learn secrets about my life? What career or person would I be when I grew up? How many children would I have? Would I get cancer and die young?" We often get involved in things because Satan even appears as an angel of light. My friend said it was just a game, but I warned her it was evil. In order to test this, one night my friend placed a Bible on the Ouija board, and it flew across the room. We were shaken up and fled upstairs. In using this example, I want you to see how we can be easily led into sin by curiosity, opening doors we were never meant to open. When sitting in front of the board, users hold a device known as a planchette and allow the "spirit" to move it around the board. Ouija boards are believed to allow spirits of the dead, usually a condemned soul or a demon, to communicate with the living; but we are warned against this throughout the Torah:

> You shall not permit a sorceress to live.
>
> −Exodus 22:18, ESV

> Do not turn to mediums or necromancers; do not seek them out, and so make yourselves unclean by them: I am the LORD your God.
>
> −Exodus 19:31, ESV

Later in my 20s, I was persuaded to see a fortune-teller who came to my job and set up a table in a restaurant/nightclub where I was working. Sin was crouching at my door, but I did not have the strength to defeat it. My fellow co-workers were telling me how the fortune teller knew everything about them, but I could hear my mother's voice in my head warning me; however, the enticement was so great, I sat at the table and had my cards read, then convinced my husband to as well. At 3 am, I walked through the door of my house from work, and my phone (before cell phones) was ringing. I picked it up, and my mother was on the line. She said, "I don't know what you been doing, but the Holy Spirit woke me up to pray for you. And I was given a dream that you were lying by a dumpster with a bunch of trash." My heart sunk. I was so ashamed. I was going through so many traumatic things that my mother knew nothing about, nor anyone else, and I had been drifting away from the Lord gradually over time and in an abusive marriage.

The fortune teller had refused to read the last card she flipped over until I told her I had paid her to read every card and she would tell me what it said even if it were death. She then flipped the last card over, and I will never forget what happened next. The woman with the crystal ball and tarot cards looked at me with her jet-black hair, long flowing robe, and headscarf and said, "This card represents your mother. She is a very powerful woman!" Even the Tarot card reader knew how powerful my mother was.

Many times, due to our upbringing or perhaps being raised in a home with drugs, alcohol, sexual abuse, verbal abuse, adding witchcraft or Tarot cards, crystals, tea leaves, Ouija boards, etc., we can become trapped in asking everyone but the Creator of all for advice and direction for our lives. Instead, we seek the darkness and not the light. Suppose a person were raised with a verbally abusive parent, a sexually abusive parent, stepparent, witchcraft, etc. In that case, they might have a great deal of fear concerning Satan, when in all actuality, it is unhealed trauma and abuse that has been carried into the next generation.

Yes, there is a spirit realm and many who have dabbled in it have become oppressed or even possessed by demons. For a year I was involved in deliverance ministry. I have witnessed people throwing up, foaming, making guttural noises, hissing, and more. In Book One of this Series, *Satan Unmasked*, I wanted to show another side of our adversary in order to bring balance to an area that often is unbalanced.

The concept of Satan has evolved over time and has become larger than life in many Christian circles. The adversary is known as the lying serpent, the prince and power of the air, as well as a dragon and devil. This concept of an evil fallen angel has grown into a fearful deity whose main job description is to wreak havoc on those trying to live righteously. In certain circles, Satan is a main topic met with remedies and formulas for how to deal with him. In the more charismatic arenas, Satan is commanded through prayer and authority to flee, bow, and be reminded that he has no power to touch their bloodline through Yeshua Messiah.

Other Christians rally on the side of James chapter 4: "Resist the devil, and he will flee from you" (James 4:7, BSB). However, when James 4 is read in full, the "devil" or adversary is the person staring back at us in the mirror:

> What causes quarrels and what causes fights among you?

Is it not this, that your passions are at war within you? You desire and do not have, so you murder. You covet and cannot obtain, so you fight and quarrel. You do not have, because you do not ask. You ask and do not receive, because you ask wrongly, to spend it on your passions. You adulterous people! Do you not know that friendship with the world is enmity with God?

–James 4:1-4, ESV

Back in the 1970s, a variety show called *Flip Wilson* brought humor to the desires of our flesh by coining the term "*the devil made me do it.*" Geraldine (one of the characters Wilson often portrayed) was forever getting into trouble for gossip, flirting with a married man, or some type of sinful nature. Comic Wilson, while dressed as Geraldine and playing the part would yell with great conviction that the devil had made her do whatever it was she knew was wrong. While in stand-up comedy this can be humorous, it's not humorous in real life.

Satan and his minions have been picking up speed and girth like a snowball headed down hill for centuries. Many in leadership believe that Satan and his cohorts are bent on destroying the righteous by attacking them and their seed. In fact, in most Christian circles Satan is often treated as a being almost equal to God in power. In Christianity, Satan has evolved into God's adversary, a fallen angel. However, in Psalms and the Book of Job, Satan is likened to a prosecuting attorney in the Heavenly Court.

The writers of the Bible were Hebrews. Judaism is monotheistic. There is only one God with authority. As Isaiah proclaims, the Holy One is the creator of both good and evil, and man is given freedom to choose which path he will follow. "I form the light, and create darkness; I make peace, and create evil. I am Jehovah, that doeth all these things" (Isaiah 45:7, ASV). Paul's letter to the Colossians declares that there is only One Elohim and by Him all things were made. In Isaiah 54, the Holy One states that He "created the waster to destroy."

> See, I Myself have created the blacksmith who blows the coals in the fire, who brings forth an instrument for his work. And I have created the waster to destroy.
>
> –Isaiah 54:16, ISR

> Who is the likeness of the invisible Elohim, the first-born of all creation. Because in Him were created all that are in the heavens and that are on earth, visible and invisible, whether thrones or rulerships or principalities or authorities – all have been created through Him and for Him. And He is before all, and in Him all hold together.
>
> –Colossians 1:15-17, ISR

Countless theologians and scholars have written about this larger-than-life enemy. *Satan Unmasked* will cover multiple passages of the Bible concerning Satan and the origins of how he crept into our doctrines and belief systems. I have included the passages of scripture from both the Old Testament (Tanakh) and the New Testament where the word Satan is used and the context of each passage as bookends. The Old Testament passages referring to Satan appear in chapter one with commentary, and the New Testament mentions of Satan, with commentary, are listed at the end of the book before the closing.

Also, in Hebrew there is no such concept of Satan being the embodiment of evil. If this concept is true, when and how did these dogmas creep into Christianity, and why do we at times feel as if the hounds of hell are on our trail? I will cover these questions and more in Book One *Satan Unmasked* and Book Two, *Spirits Unveiled,* and further in Book Three and Four regarding generational curses. Read the whole series for a full meal.

Let's dig in, shall we?

Chapter 1

Satan in the Old Testament

The noun *Satan* occurs 27 times in the Hebrew Bible (Old Testament). The definition for the word *Satan* is Strong's Hebrew 7854 meaning an adversary. In the Book of Job, Satan appears as a member of the courts who makes suggestions concerning Job's life and his character, but ultimately Satan takes orders from Adonai and is told to spare Job's life. Although the Book of Job is the oldest manuscript in the Old Testament, starting with Genesis and moving forward, the Book of Numbers is the first reference of the word *Satan* used as an adversary. Below is a list of every occurrence of the word *Satan* found in the Old Testament (Tanakh):

1. And the wrath of God was provoked against him because he went, and the Angel of LORD JEHOVAH stood in the road to be Satan, an adversary to him, and he rode on his donkey and his two young men with him.

    –Numbers 22:22, AB

The Holy One is the adversary or *Satan* in Numbers 22:22. This is not a fallen angel; this is an angel sent by the Holy One to be a Satan or adversary to Balaam.:

2. Then the angel of the LORD said to him, "Why have you struck your donkey these three times? Behold, I have come out as an adversary, because your way was reckless and contrary to me.

—Numbers 22:32, NASB

3. Concerning David, "But the princes of the Philistines were angry with him; so the princes of the Philistines said to him, "Make this fellow (David while fleeing Saul) return, that he may go back to the place which you have appointed for him, and do not let him go down with us to battle, lest in the battle he become our adversary.'"

—I Samuel 29:4, KJV

4. And David replied, "Sons of Zeruiah, what have I to do with you, that you should be my adversaries today?"

—II Samuel 19:22, KJV

5. Solomon speaks concerning adversaries, "But now the LORD my God hath given me rest on every side, so that there is neither adversary nor evil occurrent."

—I Kings 5:4, KJV

6. The Holy One sends the adversary (Satan) in I Kings 11:14:

   And the LORD stirred up an adversary unto Solomon, Hadad the Edomite; he was of the king's seed in Edom.

   –I Kings 11:14, KJV

7. The Holy One sends more adversaries concerning Solomon, "And God stirred him up another adversary, Rezon the son of Eliadah, which fled from his lord Hadadezer king of Zobah: And he gathered men unto him, and became captain over a band, when David slew them of Zobah: and they went to Damascus, and dwelt therein, and reigned in Damascus. And he was an adversary to Israel all the days of Solomon, beside the mischief that Hadad did: and he abhorred Israel and reigned over Syria."

   –I Kings 11:23-25, KJV

8. And Satan stood up against Israel, and provoked David to number Israel.

   –I Chronicles 21:1, KJV

   In II Samuel concerning I Chronicles; the adversary is the Holy One:

And again the anger of the LORD was kindled against Israel, and he (Jehovah) moved David against them to say, Go, number Israel and Judah.

–II Samuel 24:1, KJV

9. Now there was a day when the sons of God came to present themselves before the LORD, and Satan came also among them.

–Job 1:6, KJV

10. And the LORD said unto Satan, Whence comest thou?

–Job 1:7, KJV

11. Then Satan answered the LORD, and said, From going to and fro in the earth, and from walking up and down in it.

–Job 1:7, KJV

See #18, Page 5.

12. And the LORD said unto Satan, Hast thou considered my servant Job, that there is none like him in the earth, a perfect and an upright man, one that feareth God, and escheweth evil?

–Job 1:8, KJV

See #19, Page 6.

13. Then Satan answered the LORD, and said, Doth Job fear God for nought?

−Job 1:9, KJV

14. And the LORD said unto Satan, Behold, all that he hath is in thy power; only upon himself put not forth thine hand.

−Job 1:12, KJV

The Holy One allows and gives permission to Satan (the adversary):

15. So Satan went forth from the presence of the LORD.

−Job 1:12, KJV

16. Again there was a day when the sons of God came to present themselves before the LORD, and Satan came also among them to present himself before the LORD.

−Job 2:1, KJV

17. And the LORD said unto Satan, From whence comest thou?

−Job 2:2, KJV

18. And Satan answered the LORD, and said, From going to and fro in the earth, and from walking up and down in it.

−Job 2:2, KJV

See #11, Page 4.

19. And the LORD said unto Satan, Hast thou considered my servant Job, that there is none like him in the earth, a perfect and an upright man, one that feareth God, and escheweth evil? and still he holdeth fast his integrity, although thou movedst me against him, to destroy him without cause.

–Job 2:3, KJV

See #12, Page 4.

20. And Satan answered the LORD, and said, Skin for skin, yea, all that a man hath will he give for his life.

–Job 2:4, KJV

21. And the LORD said unto Satan, Behold, he is in thine hand; but save his life.

–Job 2:6, KJV

Again, authority is given from the Holy One:

22. So went Satan forth from the presence of the LORD, and smote Job with sore boils from the sole of his foot unto his crown.

–Job 2:7, KJV

The Book of Job ends and explains who was in control and allowed this suffering and adversity:

And the Lord restored Job's losses when he prayed for his friends. Indeed the Lord gave Job twice as much as he had before. Then all his brothers, all his sisters, and all those who had been his acquaintances before, came to him and ate food with him in his house; and they consoled him and comforted him for all the adversity that the Lord had brought upon him.

–Job 42:10-11, KJV

23. Set thou a wicked man over him: and let Satan stand at his right hand.

–Psalm 109:6, KJV

Psalm 109, penned by David, is a cry against his enemies, and David said he had more enemies than the hairs of his head. Besides King Saul and his armies chasing him down to kill him, one of his sons usurped him and plotted to take the throne and murder him. David describes one of his rivals as a close, familiar friends:

They say, "A deadly thing is poured out on him;
he will not rise again from where he lies."
Even my close friend in whom I trusted,
who ate my bread, has lifted his heel against me.

But you, O LORD, be gracious to me,

and raise me up, that I may repay them!

> –Psalm 41:8-10, ESV

Psalms 109 and Psalms 41 are quoted concerning Judas in Acts I:

> And in those days Peter stood up in the midst of the disciples, and said, (the number of names together were about a hundred and twenty) Men and brethren, this scripture must needs have been fulfilled, which the Holy Ghost by the mouth of David spake before concerning Judas, which was guide to them that took Jesus. For he was numbered with us, and had obtained part of this ministry. Now this man purchased a field with the reward of iniquity; and falling headlong, he burst asunder in the midst, and all his bowels gushed out. And it was known unto all the dwellers at Jerusalem; insomuch as that field is called in their proper tongue, Aceldama, that is to say, the field of blood. For it is written in the Book of Psalms, Let his habitation be desolate, and let no man dwell therein: and his bishopric let another take.
>
> –Acts 1:15-20, KJV

24. And the LORD said unto Satan, "The LORD rebuke thee, O Satan; even the LORD that hath chosen Jerusalem rebuke thee: is not this a brand plucked out of the fire?"

–Zechariah 3:2, KJV

Pelaia, Ariela, author and scholar explains more concerning the adversary in Zechariah 3 and the Book of Job in his blog *How Satan Is Viewed in Judaism:*

> Satan appears as a proper being only twice in the whole of the Hebrew Bible, in the Book of Job and in the Book of Zechariah (3:1–2). In both of these instances, the term that appears is *ha'Satan*, with *ha* being the definite article *the*. This is meant to show that the terminology is referring to a being. However, this being differs greatly from the character found in Christian or Islamic thought known as Satan or the Devil. [1]

All scripture using the term Satan found in the New Testament can be found at the closing of this book. Scriptures using serpent, dragon, devil, etc. are not included. I pray the commentary written here is helpful.

---

[1] https://www.learnreligions.com/jewish-view-of-Satan-2076775

Chapter 2

A BODY DIVIDED

Christianity is the world's largest religion, with approximately 2.4 billion believers worldwide. The Church or Body of Messiah has become entangled in man-made doctrines and points of contention for centuries. These disagreements concerning salvation and baptism, among other theological views, have caused many schisms. According to the Center for Global Christianity at Gordon-Conwell Theological Seminary, the current estimate is 47,000 denominations (2020). [2] The Catholic Church, also known as the Roman Catholic Church, is the largest worldwide. Why are there so many denominations and non-denominations?

> Between denominations, theologians, and comparative religionists, there are considerable disagreements about which groups can be appropriately called Christian, disagreements arising primarily from doctrinal differences between groups.
>
> –pewforum.org

---

[2] Status-of-Global-Christianity-2022.pdf (gordonconwell.edu)

Ironically, all these groups have the exact text: The Bible. Each sect or denomination believes they have truth where the others err.

Since birth and throughout my life, I have attended some form of church. Most, if not all, of the congregations I attended over the years had the same operating model. Besides a few differences in leadership, gifting, music, and healing, the structures were mostly the same. The central belief taught is God sent His Son to die on a cross for our sins. Multiple theologians told me that God is a good God, and the devil is a bad devil. The crux of the matter implied all the God-fearing people who are saved and baptized die and go to heaven, and all the wicked people die and go to a burning lake of fire and endure torture forever with Satan and his cohorts. If a person were born in Cambodia, a country with over fourteen million people, and were shown since birth the religion of Buddhism, which 95% of the population practices, are they just doomed for destruction? If the Jewish people do not see the Messiah in the New Testament or believe Yeshua walked this earth over 2,000 years ago, again, is salvation hopeless?

I was taught that everything evil comes from Satan, although the prophet Isaiah speaks differently: "I form the light, and create darkness: I make peace, and create evil: I the LORD do all these things" (Isaiah 45:7, KJV).

When confronted by his wife, Job says this:

But he said to her, "You speak as one of the foolish women would speak. Shall we receive good from God, and shall we not receive evil?" In all this Job did not sin with his lips.

–Job 2:10, ESV

According to multiple doctrines taught, Satan is a fallen angel who God created and placed in authority. I was taught Satan, or the Devil, was gifted to play the musical pipes and fell due to his pride. One-third of the angels sided with Satan, but I was assured by multiple theologians that none of them would ever want to be more powerful than the Holy One again. This usurping angelic coup was apparently a one-time event. The verses used to support these doctrines come from Ezekiel, Isaiah, Daniel, and Revelation. However, in the Hebrew perspective, Satan means to be or act as an adversary.

For a season, I worked in the deliverance ministry with a pastor from Africa. During that time, I met with individuals who struggled with many forms of addiction and suffering. I watched as the Lord opened doors for me to minister to a variety of sheep of all ages and from all backgrounds; and in my spare time, I devoured His Word. I began to question certain doctrines that I had been taught. At times, from the pulpit, different scriptures were used in a way that changed the truth of the Holy One's Word significantly. I heard the Father whisper to me time and again, "That is not sound teaching."

Shortly after much prayer concerning the truth of His Word, I had a dream that left me in awe. I prayed and asked the Father to give me revelation. In the dream, there appeared a Caucasian man who was Hulk-like, broad-shouldered and in cartoon character form. He was wearing a suit and tie and had a smile as broad as his shoulders. Out of his chest was another head of a man of African descent—both heads talked. The context of the dream was black and white, no grey areas. The backdrop for this vision was a morning show aired in the streets of a large city that looked like New York. In front of the announcer interviewing the gentleman with two heads was a conveyor belt coming out of a stone oven; on the conveyor belt were silver trays with delectable foods. As the smoke rose off the dainty little treats, the announcer held the microphone in front of the large man and said, "I can smell the fresh thyme, rosemary, and garlic, it smells magnificent!"

Both heads spoke in agreement, and then the announcer replied, "And you say it's all made with human dung?" "That's right," the men agreed, "and they never know it. The people just eat it up and never suspect a thing!" The announcer said, "Amazing. Well, you heard it here first people, now back to you, Rita."

I awoke and prayed until the Holy One revealed to me that these cartoon characters represented shepherds (ministers) who were taking the Word of God and making it look good, smell good, and taste good. Still, through ignorance, these leaders were feeding the people a load of crap by twisting and manipulating the Bible. Ironically, silver represents redemption, but the serving tray of silver in my dream held dung and not the bread of life to free those being held captive. I believe most ministers mean well but are simply passing down what they had been taught through ignorance. My earthly father had passed it down to me, and I had passed it down to others. "Our fathers have inherited nothing but lies, worthless things in which there is no profit" (Jeremiah 16:19, ESV).

Adolph Hitler quoted Joseph Goebbels when he said, "If you tell a big enough lie and tell it frequently enough, it will be believed." [3] Plato, Socrates, and Aristotle's Greek doctrinal influence have trickled into our church houses for over two thousand years. By the first century, the religious culture of Israel had nearly 400 years of Hellenized practice. Many theologians with good intentions have told us the same lies taught to them. We have all heard doctrines that did not add up, but we have listened to them so frequently that we have accepted these lies as truth, often never researching the Holy One's Word with a mind free of preconceived notions.

Once we are taught a particular way of doing something, it is hard to reverse it. New wine placed in old skins causes the skins to burst. I drove a five-speed Mitsubishi for years. After it died, I

---

[3] https://www.inspiringquotes.us/quotes/TzEs_7CxEctuv

bought an automatic, but my foot still pushed down on the imaginary clutch. It is the same with dogmas. Once we have heard Biblical passages strung along and placed in a specific order, that is all we know. We become so accustomed to how the teaching was presented to us that changing its structure appears shameful. Paul explains more:

> I give you this charge: Preach the word; be prepared in season and out of season; correct, rebuke, and encourage with great patience and careful instruction. For the time will come when people will not put up with sound doctrine. Instead, to suit their own desires, they will gather around them a great number of teachers to say what their itching ears want to hear. They will turn their ears away from the truth and turn aside to myths.
>
> –II Timothy 4:1-4, KJV

Paul instructs Timothy to remain in Ephesus to combat erroneous doctrines. Two grievous problems with the false teachers in Ephesus were myths and genealogies. In this context, *myths* are traditions not found in the Scriptures. These doctrinal myths add to or contradict biblical instruction. Not all traditions are bad, but those which are contrary to or twist the Word are bad:

> But we should always thank God for you, brothers who are loved by the Lord, because God has chosen you from the beginning to be saved by the sanctification of the Spirit

and by faith in the truth. To this He called you through our gospel, so that you may share in the glory of our Lord Jesus Christ. Therefore, brothers, stand firm and cling to the traditions we taught you, whether by speech or by letter.

–II Thessalonians 2:13-15, BSB

Having been raised and educated under the Assemblies of God doctrines, even as a young girl, I was taught things that disturbed me. The ministers from my youth proclaimed authority to summon angels at their command, rebuke every sickness, and scream at demons they felt controlled everything. These ministers in leadership seemed to have power overall, including whether a person prospered or not. One man could pray for wealth and favor to be transferred; all the person had to do was give money to his ministry or plant a seed, as he called it. Another could break every generational curse brought by Satan on a family. Many of these men boasted about their airplanes or how many millions with which the Father had blessed them. In II Timothy 4, we learn of men who wanted their ears tickled:

For the time will come when men will not tolerate sound doctrine, but with itching ears they will gather around themselves teachers to suit their own desires. So they will turn their ears away from the truth and turn aside to myths.

–II Timothy 4:3-4, BSB

This type of "itching ear" teaching began to grow stronger in the United States in the early 1940s. By the 1990s, the prosperity gospel had gone full circle, spreading across the globe swiftly. Motivational teachings appeal to our human desire to be successful, healthy, and prosperous. It screams, "Live your best life and speak positive words." There is nothing wrong with speaking life or positive words, but these teachings are often unbalanced, focusing on our fleshly desires, emotionalism, and not our inner condition. Norman Vincent Peale (1898–1993), the pastor of Marble Collegiate Church in New York City, popularized the doctrine of positive thinking and self-focus with his book *The Power of Positive Thinking* (1952). The first chapter of Peale's book is titled *Believe in Yourself.* This type of doctrine makes the reader believe that if they have a positive attitude and speak words of affirmation, nothing terrible will happen to them. The Bible makes it clear that the troubles we experience in this life are not simply the outcome of negative thinking. Insinuating we can overcome by tapping into our potential through positive thinking when in all actuality, we can overcome by the blood of the Lamb and our testimony:

> And they have overcome him by reason of the blood of the Lamb, and by reason of the word of their testimony; and they have not loved their life unto death.
>
> –Revelation 12:11, BLB

Author and teacher Russell S. Woodbridge from the *Gospel Coalition* explores the dangers of the prosperity gospel movement in his blog *Prosperity Gospel Born in the USA*. Woodbridge covers one of the founders of the prosperity doctrine, a man named E.W. Kenyon, who led the way for Kenneth Hagin, Kenneth Copeland, Frederick Price, and Robert Tilton, among others:

> One can discern some of the key recurring elements of the prosperity gospel: speaking the right words, invoking a universal law of success with words, and having faith in oneself. The ideas of New Thought influenced, among others, E. W. Kenyon (1867–1948), an evangelist, pastor, and founder of *Bethel Bible Institute*. His approach to theology is the basis for one of the prosperity gospel's most distinctive features—speaking the right words to bring about a new reality; what you confess, you possess. Kenyon served as a link to the popular prosperity preachers that formed the foundation of the modern prosperity gospel movement. [4]

However, this "name it and claim it" theology did not concern only prosperity. During my earlier years, I can recall sitting in the pew and hearing ministers pray with authority over spirits, sickness, and every demon that had come to torment the person standing before them. Yet, despite all their binding and

---

[4] https://www.thegospelcoalition.org/article/prosperity-gospel-born-in-the-usa/

loosing, my mother remained sick. She suffered for years and was prayed over by some of the biggest names on the scene. Still, my mother was plagued with Parkinson's disease and other ailments. She went on to die after colon cancer surgery, contracting Clostridium difficile or C. diff, a bacterial infection while in the hospital. My mother was a woman who did ministry, worked the prayer line, handed out tracts, and told people about Yeshua often.

As I grew older, more and more doctrines crept into the church from well-known evangelists and television ministers. One night in my early thirties, I decided I wanted to know what the Bible said for myself. I no longer wanted to go to church on Saturday or Sunday and take what one man behind a pulpit taught me as truth.

Learning became a passion for me. And it started with a reverence for the Holy One:

> He has commanded mankind: To fear the Lord—that is wisdom; to move away from evil—that is understanding.
>
> –Job 28:28, ISV

After a personal life encounter, I went swiftly to work researching the Bible concerning sickness, spirits, and Satan. I sought to search and fully investigate His Word. I also wanted to comprehend why my praying mother had become mentally tormented and diagnosed with Lewy Body Dementia, a form of Parkinson's disease. Was this suffering a demon of darkness?

Was this a curse on my family? Why didn't any of the tactics used in the church bring restoration, healing, or peace? Why didn't binding and loosing work?

On this journey, I discovered many different denominations had accepted strange doctrines of men having their own set of rules and formulas for victory. It made me speculate and ask who had the correct theology. Even the Roman Catholic Church, which claims to be undivided, is now disagreeing on divorce and birth control, among other topics. Why were there no Christian denominations in the Bible? Wasn't Yeshua a Jew? How can people be sure their faith is teaching the absolute truth? And why was there so much finger-pointing? Why did Yeshua say, "I am not sent but unto the lost sheep of the house of Israel" (Matthew 15:24, KJV)? Who are these sheep? One of the common claims among the followers of the Messianic movement is that those who are now discovering their Hebrew roots are part of the "lost tribes of Israel," but is this true? Is salvation a one-time prayer said with a pastor or in private?

This four-part book series will examine topics that have divided the Body of Believers for some time now. Remember, that number reaches almost 50,000 Christian sects alone. Sadly, many of the false doctrines from our past have found their way into the Christian community, and the Messianic and Torah communities. After reading Book One, *Satan Unmasked*, you will better understand Adonai, His creation, and the adversary, who many refer to as Satan.

Have I found new truths no one else has discovered? No, it's not new; it's ancient. It is truth found by doing an excavation. "It is the glory of God to conceal a thing; But the glory of kings is to search out a matter" (Proverbs 25:2, ASV). This type of archaeological dig involves traveling back to the 1st century and the days of the Apostles written about in the Book of Acts to uncover it.

Nevertheless, I believe some have found truths no one ever told them about at the local watering hole. Paul said:

> For I know this, that after my departure savage wolves will come in among you, not sparing the flock. Also from among yourselves men will rise up, speaking perverse things, to draw away the disciples after themselves.
>
> –Acts 20:29-30, NKJ

Join me as we uncover a plethora of erroneous tales and traits concerning the adversary, *ha-Satan*.

Chapter 3

THE SERPENT

Beginning in Genesis, we read of Adam and Eve (*Chavah*) and they are living in a garden of paradise when along comes a talking serpent. Certainly, the serpent in Genesis did not find a crack or pull a fast one on the Creator of all. We know the snake did not slip in unawares. The serpent, too, was created by the Holy One:

> But the serpent was shrewder than any animal of the field that Adonai Elohim made. So it said to the woman, "Did God really say, 'You must not eat from all the trees of the garden?'"
>
> –Genesis 3:1, TLV

The text from Genesis 3 does not call the animal an angel disguised as a serpent. The text says that Adonai created the serpent. When Adonai asked why Adam and Eve (*Chavah*) had eaten of the tree, Eve spoke up and said, "The serpent deceived me and I ate" (Genesis 3:13, TLV). Gathering information, we learn that the serpent could speak. Adonai created the serpent, and everything He created is good or used for His purposes.

In addition, in Genesis 3, we hear a dialogue between Eve (*Chavah*) and the Holy One, and something interesting happens. It is something I have never heard preached before during my church upbringing. If I were honest, I would say I have listened to just the opposite. Adonai says He is cursing the wild animal He created, and that the serpent would be cursed more than any beast. The Holy One proclaimed that the snake would reside on its belly in the dust and eat dust all its life:

> And יהוה Elohim said to the serpent, "Because you have done this, you are cursed more than all livestock and more than every beast of the field. On your belly you are to go, and eat dust all the days of your life.
>
> –Genesis 3:14, TLV

Sadly, snakes get a bad rap. Not all snakes are poisonous. We need snakes for a healthy ecosystem and a healthy environment. They keep the mice and rat population under control, among other things, but what if the serpent in the garden is not like the snake we see on the ground slithering? The Bible, and especially the Torah, the first five books of Moses, were written for a people just coming out of Egypt. The snake is commonly associated with certain gods of ancient Egypt, and the Egyptians had many gods. In order to understand the audience Moses was writing for, it's important to understand the place they had been freed from. Osiris was a god they believed would rise from the dead. Osiris's wife was said to have molded snakes or serpents out of clay.

Osiris was the god of fertility and agriculture but also resurrection. Richard H. Wilkinson, author of *The Complete Gods and Goddesses of Ancient Egypt* describes more details concerning Osiris:

> When Osiris's brother, Set, cut him up into pieces after killing him, Isis, his wife, found all the pieces and wrapped his body up, enabling him to return to life. Osiris was at times considered the eldest son of the earth god Geb and the sky goddess Nut, as well as being brother and husband of Isis, with Horus being considered his posthumously begotten son. [5]

Osiris did not return to life. He journeyed to the underworld, where he became the so-called lord of the dead. Multiple stories concerning the gods of Egypt had serpents involved in the details. Again, Isis was said to have kneaded clay into the shape of a snake. The Egyptians believed she brought the snake to life with her magical powers; the snake bit the sun god Ra. The serpent's venom flooded Ra's body like the Nile that flooded during seasonal rains. My point in sharing all of this is the God of the Bible had Moses write the Torah for a people who had been enslaved in Egypt and taught about many gods and goddesses. They were enslaved under the Pharaoh, and he wore a live serpent on his regal headdress. The serpent was the Egyptian symbol of royal authority and healing. The serpent, also referred

---

[5] https://en.wikipedia.org/wiki/Osiris

to as Satan, the devil, and a dragon in Revelation 12, describes a beastly system. A harlot system. A system ruled by men whose bellies reside in the dust and are full of their beastly nature. The Father sends a message through Ezekiel concerning Pharaoh, and notice the Holy One says Pharaoh sits as god and thinks he created the Nile:

> Because you (Pharaoh) said, 'The Nile is mine, and I have made it, 'therefore, behold, I am against you and against your canals, and I will make the land of Egypt an utter waste and desolation, from Migdol to Syene and as far as the border of Cush. A human foot will not pass through it, nor will the foot of an animal pass through it, and it will not be inhabited for forty years. So I will make the land of Egypt a desolation in the midst of deserted lands. And her cities, in the midst of cities that are laid waste, will be desolate for forty years; and I will scatter the Egyptians among the nations and disperse them among the lands.
>
> –Ezekiel 29:9-12, NASB

In Genesis 3, the Holy One states that the serpent now is cursed and will reside on his belly eating dust. If the serpent were Satan and many believe it was, and is, and that He is powerful, why did God say, ". . . you are cursed more than all livestock and more than every beast of the field. On your belly you are to go, and eat dust all the days of your life?" Notice that Adam and his wife are not cursed. The ground is cursed. The rich soil that was effortless now has become hard, and there were thorns and thistles. Adam, through great toil and sweat, will work for his food. Eve (*Chavah*) will conceive and bear children in pain. As a mother, she will worry about her seed and witness the first shedding of blood by her son Cain. Did Satan cause Cain to kill Abel? A closer look reveals Cain's lower beastly nature was the issue:

> Then the LORD said to Cain, "Why are you angry? And why is your face gloomy? If you do well, will your face not be cheerful? And if you do not do well, sin is lurking at the door; and its desire is for you, but you must master it." Cain talked to his brother Abel; and it happened that when they were in the field Cain rose up against his brother Abel and killed him.
>
> –Genesis 4:6-8, NASB

Cain was told to master his sinful nature. We never learn to master our beastly nature when all the blame for sin is placed on Satan. We see the duality of this repeatedly. Carefully picture the twins in the womb of Rebecca:

> When her days leading to the delivery were at an end, behold, there were twins in her womb. Now the first came out red, all over like a hairy garment; and they named him Esau. Afterward his brother came out with his hand holding on to Esau's heel, so he was named Jacob; and Isaac was sixty years old when she (Rebecca) gave birth to them.
>
> –Genesis 25:24-26, NASB

In the womb he (Jacob) took his brother by the heel, and
in his manhood he strove with God. He strove with the
angel and prevailed; he wept and sought his favor. He met
God at Bethel, and there God spoke with us—the LORD,
the God of hosts, the LORD is his memorial name.

–Hosea 12:3-5, ESV

This is a picture of duality and our sinful nature. Twins
resided in Rebecca's belly. One was hairy and beastly, and one
was smooth. We see this same duality concerning Cain and Abel.
The Father tells Cain that sin lurks at his door and that his sinful
nature desires to overpower his spiritual nature:

If you (Cain) do well, will you not be accepted? And if you
do not do well, sin is crouching at the door. Its desire is
contrary to you, but you must rule over it.

–Genesis 4:7, ESV

Like you and I, Cain was warned that his sinful nature, appetites,
desires, jealousy, and anger were trying to take over his spirit
man. We are told the spirit is willing, but the flesh is weak. Cain
does not blame a fallen angel for his condition or his
punishment. In the end, the Father is merciful to Cain. Again, we
see that Satan is not omnipresent, omnipotent, or omniscient. If
not careful, many will give Satan power equal to Adonai and
place the blame on him instead of looking inward:

Know therefore today, and take it to your heart, that the LORD, He is God in heaven above and on the earth below; there is no other. "So you shall keep His statutes and His commandments which I am giving you today, that it may go well with you and with your children after you, and that you may live long on the land which the LORD your God is giving you for all time.

–Deuteronomy 4:39-40, NASB

There is no God but one. These verses profess that the Lord Adonai is Lord in heaven and on earth, and there is no other.

Adonai is Master over all. Satan is not master over all, but some theologians proclaim that Satan is the god of this world. Paul's words in II Corinthians have often been used as a proof text that Satan, for now, is the god of the world:

In whose case the god of this world has blinded the minds of the unbelieving so that they might not see the light of the gospel of the glory of Christ, who is the image of God.

–II Corinthians 4:4, NASB

What kind of blindness is Paul speaking of? Who is the god of this world? We just read from the Book of Deuteronomy that the Father Elohim is God in heaven and on the earth below, and there is no other, so we must be missing something. Reading the chapter before this one from Corinthians gives the full context:

Therefore having such a hope, we use great boldness in our speech, and are not like Moses, who used to put a veil over his face so that the sons of Israel would not look intently at the end of what was fading away. But their minds were hardened; for until this very day at the reading of the old covenant the same veil remains unlifted, because it is removed in Christ. But to this day whenever Moses is read, a veil lies over their heart; but whenever a person turns to the Lord, the veil is taken away. Now the Lord is the Spirit, and where the Spirit of the Lord is, there is liberty. But we all, with unveiled face, beholding as in a mirror the glory of the Lord, are being transformed into the same image from glory to glory, just as from the Lord, the Spirit.

–II Corinthians 3:12-18, NASB

Could it be possible that the Pharisaical spirit has blinded their eyes? A veil was over their hearts and eyes. The god of Paul's world at that time was a harsh Pharisaical spirit. Many passages reveal that the Holy One has blinded eyes and shut up ears:

But even though He had performed so many signs before them, they were not trusting in Him. This was to fulfill the word of Isaiah the prophet, who said, "Adonai, who has believed our report? To whom has the arm of Adonai been revealed?" For this reason they could not believe, for Isaiah also said, "He has blinded their eyes and hardened their hearts, so they might not see with their eyes nor understand with their hearts and turn back, and I would heal them."

–John 12:37-40, TLV

Again, we read this in Isaiah 6:10, NASB:

Render the hearts of this people insensitive, their ears dull, and their eyes dim, otherwise they might see with their eyes, hear with their ears, understand with their hearts, and return and be healed.

Continuing in Luke with Yeshua's words:

To you has been given to know the secrets of the kingdom of God; but to the others it is given in parables, in order that "Seeing, they may not see, and hearing, they may not understand."

–Luke 8:10, TLV

The Holy One blinded them, but men have taught us with good intentions a different gospel.

Many in the church teach that Satan is the god of this world and that he is responsible for evil, wickedness, murder, sex trafficking, and so forth. However, Genesis reveals the true culprit:

The Lord saw that the wickedness of man was great in the earth, and that every intention of the thoughts of his heart was only evil continually. And the Lord regretted that he had made man on the earth, and it grieved him to his heart.

–Genesis 6:5-6, ESV

The passage from Genesis 6 does not imply that Adonai regretted creating a perfect cherub or archangel that fell due to pride. A careful study of scriptures informs us that the wickedness of man will be great in the last days. Yes, it will be exactly like that again on the face of the earth before Yeshua comes back. Why? Because it is our heart condition and our beastly nature that is the problem:

For out of the heart come evil thoughts, murder, adultery, sexual immorality, theft, false witness, and slander.

–Matthew 15:19, TLV

In addition to Matthew 15, the prophet Jeremiah sums up the problem without mincing a word: "The heart is deceitful above all things, and desperately sick; who can understand it?" (Jeremiah 17:9, ESV).

The scriptures often used to describe Satan as the prince or ruler of this world contradict one another and disagree. If Satan is the prince of this world, why did Yeshua say this before going to the cross? "Now is the judgment of this world! Now the prince of this world will be driven out! And as I am lifted up from the earth, I will draw all to Myself" (John 12:31-32, TLV). If the prince of this world were Satan and he were cast out at the cross, how could he still be here? If he were cast out, why would Peter warn us that the adversary roams around like a lion? (I Peter 5:8). *Yeshua* said:

> For judgment I came into this world, so that those who don't see may see, and the ones who do see may become blind.

> –John 9:39, TLV

What is Yeshua speaking of? The blind would see He was the Son of Adonai. The prince of the world during the days of Yeshua refers to the corrupt leaders--men the Messiah called vipers. Viper is an *idiom* from the first century, an insult used by others in antiquity. Many of the Pharisees and Sadducees made His Word weak. Yeshua said, "Making the word of God of none effect through your tradition" (Mark 7:13, KJV). These rulers controlled the people with their added rules and lofty positions of power. These priests tied heavy loads on men's backs. They would have to become blind to see. They were consumed with their self-righteousness and also with controlling the Sanhedrin. Political powers and corrupt rulers like Pharaoh think they created the Nile. Still, just as Yeshua reminded Pilate, he would have no power unless it was given to him by His Father:

> So Pilate said to him, "You will not speak to me? Do you not know that I have authority to release you and authority to crucify you?" Jesus answered him, "You would have no authority over me at all unless it had been

given you from above. Therefore he who delivered me over to you has the greater sin.

–John 19:10-11, ESV

After the Messiah's death and resurrection, the kingdom of heaven was now in their midst:

> Being asked by the Pharisees when the kingdom of God would come, he answered them, "The kingdom of God is not coming in ways that can be observed, nor will they say, 'Look, here it is!' or 'There!' for behold, the kingdom of God is in the midst of you.

–Luke 17:20-21, ESV

When gathering information on the adversary or terms used to describe different adversaries, we learn that the serpent might be our lower beastly nature. The adversary may be men or women in leadership who need to be delivered from self-righteousness and pride. Each verse using the term serpent, adversary, or Satan must be thoroughly examined for context and balance because, by the first century, the religious culture of Israel had nearly 400 years of Hellenized practice. Although we see little signs of the Devil and his minions in the Old Testament, there is much concerning Satan and spirits in the new portion of our Bibles. Over time, the doctrines of men have crept in and evolved, leaving the truth of Yeshua buried under ideologies and religion. It is time for a major excavation.

Chapter 4

PRINCIPALITIES AND POWERS

I once knew a lady who blamed everything rotten in her life on Satan. I witnessed her scream at her car with over two hundred thousand miles on it, "Satan, take your filthy hands off my car!" She would take her fist and pound on the dashboard repeatedly when the clutch would slip. Perhaps the car was just worn out and old from many years of service?

Not only did this woman believe Satan attacked her car, but also any appliance that refused to work and anything that seemed to bring her annoyance. If the line were too long at the store or if she forgot her PIN to her bank card, she would scream, "Satan, take your filthy hands off my mind! Satan you must bow under my authority!" I wondered how long he would stay bowed at her command.

This disturbing behavior also seemed to be present among her close circle of friends. They were forever binding demons, pleading the blood, or talking to the enemy. On more than one occasion, I overheard the names of different demons sent by the adversary to destroy these friends and sabotage their day. A stranger would have thought that they were close to being imprisoned like the apostle Paul to be put under such attacks, and yet Paul never told Satan to take his filthy paws off him, not even once.

Is everything that goes wrong in our lives due to Satan? *Ha-Satan* is usually translated as the accuser or adversary. *Ha* translates in English as *the* and is used as a title given to a being, versus the name of a being. For instance, the baker is a title of a man or woman who bakes bread, but that is not the baker's name. The mechanic is a title given to a person who works on cars but that is not the mechanic's name. What do we wrestle against?

> For we wrestle not against flesh and blood, but against principalities, against powers, against the rulers of the darkness of this world, against spiritual wickedness in high places.
>
> –Ephesians 6:12, KJV

This scripture has been used as an example of a spiritual hierarchy of demons. The word *principality* shows rulership. "Put them in mind to be subject to principalities and powers, to obey magistrates, to be ready to every good work" (Titus 3:1, KJV).

Principalities and powers are not always demons but could be our government leaders. We must first ask ourselves what the apostles were wrestling with at that time concerning leaders:

Now about that time, Herod the king laid hands on some who belonged to the church to mistreat them. And he had James the brother of John put to death with a sword.

–Acts 12:1-2, NASB

This Herod was not the same Herod that beheaded John the Baptist. That Herod was Herod Agrippa. There was another Herod at the time of the birth of Messiah who slew all the baby boys under the age of two in Bethlehem. This Herod was hoping to slaughter the Messiah. Countless verses explain why these powers and rulers of darkness were men that could not and would not stand for the Kingdom of Heaven taking over their kingdom. Acts 17 is a prime example. Lonnie Lane, teacher, author, and speaker, gives us a broader perspective into this teaching on principalities by explaining what kind of church the apostles were starting in her article *Church Isn't In the New Testament*:

> Paul and Silas were accused of "turning the world (system) upside down" (Acts 17:1-6 KJV). What was their message that made them worthy of such a declaration? Paul came to town and began proclaiming Yeshua in the Temple. Here's what then took place: " . . . becoming jealous and taking along some wicked men from the marketplace, (some) formed a mob and set the city in an uproar; and attacking the house of Jason, they were seeking to bring them out to the people. When they did not find them, they began

dragging Jason and some brethren before the city authorities, shouting, "These men who have upset the world have come here also." What was the message that was so enflaming? The accusation is found in the next verse: "and Jason has welcomed them, and they all act contrary to the decrees of Caesar, saying that there is another king, Yeshua" (vs. 7).

They weren't telling the people to start a church, find a building and a minister, attend every weekend, and act like good "Christians." That wouldn't have incited the city fathers against them. No, they were announcing another king other than Caesar. They were calling people out of the Roman system into another Kingdom -- God's Kingdom -- a Kingdom far more powerful than Caesar's, an entirely alternative life and allegiance. A whole new identity and way of life. These would now be people who no longer looked to Caesar as their king. This would have been seen as a declaration of war, of treason. Such is the way of the "called out ones." [6]

Lane explains that Paul and Silas's words were freeing the people from the mental holds of the aristocrats in positions of high places. The people were taught that Rome was the exalted government and Caesar was a god along with all the Roman and

---

[6] https://sidroth.org/articles/church-isnt-new-testament/

Greek gods. The message of Paul and Silas was freeing them from bondage and chains. They, too, could be a part of a kingdom, an everlasting kingdom of Messiah Yeshua, and the called-out ones.

We have spiritual wickedness in high places in multiple nations today. Paul was more than likely referring to the powers that be and the very ones who had thrown him in a prison cell where he wrote these words:

> For we wrestle not against flesh and blood, but against principalities, against powers, against the rulers of the darkness of this world, against spiritual wickedness in high places.

> –Ephesians 6:12, KJV

Since our Messiah died and rose again, He is now seated at the Right Hand of the Father in the heavens, far above all principalities. Our Messiah is far above these fleshly men in positions of authority on earth:

> And what is the exceeding greatness of his power to usward who believe, according to the working of his mighty power, which he wrought in Christ, when he raised him from the dead, and set him at his own right hand in the heavenly places, far above all principality, and power, and might, and dominion, and every name that is named, not only in this world but also in that which is to come. And hath put all things under his feet and gave him to be the head over all

things to the church [assembly].

–Ephesians 1:19-23, KJV

Yeshua, the Messiah, is over every world leader. He is head over all rule and authority. This passage from Ephesians I is not about invisible demonic forces but rulers and authorities who may have power to throw Paul in prison or crucify him, but they have no power over the resurrection of the dead and eternal life through Messiah. The Messiah is above all principalities and powers and dominion because He is the Word made flesh. He is the Lamb that was slain and received the keys to death, hell, and the grave. The word *principality* is Strong's Hebrew 4761 *marashah*, and it means headship. When they came to arrest Yeshua, He spoke these words:

> My kingdom is not of this world. If My kingdom were of this world, then My servants would be fighting so that I would not be handed over to the Jews; but as it is, My kingdom is not of this realm.

–John 18:36, NASB

Rethinking principalities and powers is needed to discern the context of specific passages like Ephesians chapter I and specifically Ephesians 6:12. Before He was crucified, Yeshua spoke to Pilate and explained the power given to Pilate came from His Father. "You would have no authority over me at all unless it had been given you from above. Therefore he who delivered me over to you has the greater sin" (John 19:11, ESV).

Demonic strongholds may influence those in positions of earthly authority, but ultimately, we know that Adonai is in control of all things.

Chapter 5

WHO IS SATAN?

Multiple imageries concerning the appearance of Satan have emerged over time. Hollywood and the entertainment industry often depict Satan in a bright red suit with horns growing out of his head. This representation comes from the Greek god Pan. The cult of Pan continued well into the 4th Century CE and beyond. The image of Pan gave birth to the physical appearance of what we call Satan or the Devil. Ironically, in Greek mythology, Pan was the god of shepherds and flocks. He also was gifted with reed pipes and had a goatee. From the waist down, he had a goat's body and also the sexual habits of a goat. The Greek god Neptune was portrayed with a trident which evolved into a pitchfork. The apostle Paul warns that Satan does not appear to us with this ghastly form.

Then, how can something evil appear to us as an Angel of Light? "And no wonder, for even Satan disguises himself as an angel of light" (II Corinthians 11:14, ESV). Those who know the Father intimately can see the world's corruption. They are not blinded to wickedness but are grieved just as Lot was:

He rescued Lot, a righteous man deeply troubled by the

shameless immorality of the wicked. (For that righteous man, while living among them, was tormented in his righteous soul day after day by lawless deeds he saw and heard.)

–II Peter 2:7-8, TLV

The angel of light often comes through those who proclaim to be followers of Messiah, or through our own thoughts and desires.

The Jewish people do not believe in Satan as an enemy of our Father but as a servant. This idea is due to the translators and errors in scriptural teachings. In II Samuel 21 and I Chronicles 21, the same story is being told but with conflicting messages. In II Samuel 24:1, the Lord is the adversary against David, and in I Chronicles 21:1, Satan is the adversary tempting David:

Then Satan stood up against Israel and moved David to number Israel.

–I Chronicles 21:1, NASB

Now again, the anger of the LORD burned against Israel, and it incited David against them to say, "Go, number Israel and Judah."

–II Samuel 24:1, NASB

As stated in previous chapters, the word *Satan* is a title and not a name. Satan means an enemy or opponent. The Hebrew term *Satan* is one who accuses, in the legal sense of a district attorney who brings charges before a court. The original translation of the 1611 *King James Version* of Numbers 22 reveals more:

> And Balaam arose in the morning, saddled his donkey, and went with the rulers of Moab. And God's anger burned because he went, and the Angel of Jehovah stationed Himself in the way as Satan against him.

> –Numbers 22:21-22, KJV-1611

The Older Testament or *Tanakh* uses the word *devil* as a hairy goat. It is *Strong's Hebrew Concordance* 8163. *sa'iyr* meaning hairy, goat. Leviticus 17:7 is one example of this:

> And they shall no more offer their sacrifices unto devils, after whom they have gone a whoring. This shall be a statute for ever unto them throughout their generations.

> –Leviticus 17:7, KJV

JPS Tanakh 1917 uses the word *satyrs*. Other newer translations say goat *demons*. Other points of reference are Deuteronomy 32:17, II Chronicles 11:15, and Psalms 106:37. The 1917 translation is in place of (goat-like idols) pagan rituals. The Septuagint says demons. The verses do not refer to an entity or evil being called Satan. *Keil and Delitzsch Biblical Commentary* on the Old Testament states:

> The Seirim were the gods whom the Israelites worshipped and went a whoring after in Egypt (Joshua 24:14; Ezekiel

20:7; Ezekiel 23:3, Ezekiel 23:8, Ezekiel 23:19, Ezekiel 23:21, Ezekiel 23:27). Both the thing and the name were derived from the Egyptians, who worshipped goats as gods, particularly Pan, who was represented in the form of a goat, a personification of the male and fertilizing principle in nature, whom they called Mendes and reckoned among the eight leading gods, and to whom they had built a splendid and celebrated temple in Thmuis, the capital of the Mendesian Nomos in Lower Egypt, and erected statues in the temples in all directions (cf. Herod. 2, 42, 46; Strabo, xvii. 802; Diod. Sic. i. 18). [7]

Culture is a huge factor in what we believe is true about the world and demonic entities. We must read the Bible in its own context and understand how the world looked to people in that time period. In some cultures, demons and devils are actually the mentally ill or those with a disability. Not everything is evil but instead may be functioning out of divine order.

Paul in Colossians 1:16-17 states that all things were created by the Lord and for Him. If Adonai or His Son Yeshua created everything, how did evil get here?

> I form the light, and create darkness, I make peace and create evil: I the Lord do all these things!
>
> –Isaiah 45:7, KJV

---

[7] : https://biblehub.com/commentaries/leviticus/17-7.htm

Who can speak and have it happen if the Lord has not decreed it? Out of the mouth of the Most High proceedeth not evil and good?

–Lamentations 3:37-38, KJV

The Father disciplines the one he loves, and he chastens everyone he accepts as his son.

–Hebrews 12:6, KJV

The Old Testament never treats Satan as a specific being. Yet, we tend to blame attacks on Satan instead of seeing them as the Lord's hand. Instead of recognizing that repentance is needed or that chastening happens to believers when they are disobedient, we look for an outward force. What a tragedy. Dr. Skip Moen, author, teacher, and Hebrew scholar has a fascinating article entitled *Essenes, Rabbis, and Christians*, which gives more information on Satan and the evolution thereof:

> In the Tanakh, ha-Satan is more like an office in the heavenly court, an adversary whose job is to raise questions about human loyalty and obedience. The word is used of actual human persons, not just divine figures. But by the time Hellenism had penetrated the thinking of the Mediterranean world, all of this changed.
>
> In the Qumran documents, "The angel of darkness is the same as Belial elsewhere, whom God has created with whom he is in conflict, who oppresses the righteous, and

who will finally be judged. The term satan occurs in the Scrolls only three times in obscure connections." In later Judaism, "The rabbis suggest that the devil is a fallen angel, although Qumran finds no place for this view." [8]

Everything is under Adonai's jurisdiction. Satan is not a rival of Adonai but more like a go-between, sent to do what the Father would have done. We see an example of this in the story of Joseph. Joseph's brothers were jealous of him and threw him in a pit as a satan against him. His brothers sold him into Egypt. The Holy One used their actions to achieve the plans He already had for Joseph. After Joseph's brothers arrive in Egypt and become aware of his identity, Joseph tells them the Lord used all their actions for good:

> I am your brother, Joseph, whom you sold into Egypt. And now do not be distressed or angry with yourselves because you sold me here, for God sent me before you to preserve life.
>
> –Genesis 45:8, ESV

---

[8] https://skipmoen.com/2019/06/essenes-rabbis-and-christians/

Chapter 6

THE SATAN IN THE MIRROR

Three of the Gospels written in the New Testament give accounts of Yeshua Messiah being led into the wilderness to be tempted by the adversary. "Then Jesus was led up by the Spirit into the wilderness to be tempted by the devil" (Matthew 4:1, ESV). Mark I exclaims the Holy Spirit drove or impelled Yeshua into the wilderness. "The Spirit immediately drove him out into the wilderness" (Mark 1:12, ESV). Yeshua spent 40 days in the wilderness before He began His earthly ministry. The number 40 is incredibly significant in the Bible. The number 40 often represents transition or change. After 40 years, Moses was called to lead the Children of Israel out of Egypt. Moses spent 40 days on the mountain several times seeking the Father. God's people arrived at Mt. Sinai as a nation who had been enslaved, but after 40 days, they were transformed and given their wedding vows. On the 40th day of the Omer Count, Yeshua ascended into heaven:

In the first book, O Theophilus, I have dealt with all that Jesus began to do and teach, until the day when he was taken up, after he had given commands through the Holy Spirit to the apostles whom he had chosen. He presented himself alive to them after his suffering by many proofs, appearing to them during forty days and speaking about the kingdom of God.

–Acts 1:1-3, ESV

The disciples were counting up to the number 49/50, looking towards the next feast day called Pentecost in Christianity or Shavuot in Hebrew:

From the day after the Sabbath, the day you brought the sheaf of the wave offering, you are to count off seven full weeks. You shall count off fifty days until the day after the seventh Sabbath, and then present an offering of new grain to the LORD.

–Leviticus 23:15-16, BSB

The Hebrew letter *mem* is the 13th letter of the alphabet (Hebrew alphabet,) and means water. Hebrew letters have a numerical value. *Mem* has a numerical value of 40. After forty days, the embryo of a child begins to assume a recognizable form, and after 40 weeks, the child in the womb is fully developed. The number 40 is similar to a supernatural metamorphosis. According to *Hebrew Today:*

The numerical value of the letter מ (mem) is 40. This number represents ripeness and maturity. This is because according to Jewish tradition, 40 days after conception, a fetus begins to take on human form.

The ideal full life for a person is 120 years (based on the life of Moses), which splits into three segments of 40 years. Each segment is a stage of different stage development in a person's life. 9

Yeshua was led into the wilderness for 40 days.

Before Yeshua began his ministry, he had to go heel to heel with His flesh nature and defeat the adversary who brought temptation after temptation. Sometimes our trials and test are Holy Spirit ordained: "Then was Jesus led up of the spirit the wilderness to be tempted of the devil" (Matthew 4:1, KJV). The devil or adversary did not hunt down Yeshua and begin tempting Him. Yeshua was led by the Holy Spirit (the *Ruach Ha-Kodesh* in Hebrew). Yeshua overcame the adversary by quoting from the Torah, the Book of Deuteronomy. The Book of *Devarim*, or Deuteronomy, means *words*. Yeshua used His Father's Words given to Moses to defeat the enemy. Our Messiah felt our weaknesses:

For we do not have a high priest who is unable to sympathize with our weaknesses, but we have one who

---

9 The Letter Mem (מ) - Hebrew Today

was tempted in every way that we are, yet was without sin. Let us then approach the throne of grace with confidence, so that we may receive mercy and find grace to help us in our time of need.

–Hebrews 4:15-16, BSB

Paul highlights the testing our Messiah went through and how He is more human than we know. Only someone who has shared in our sufferings can be helpful when we are suffering. Yeshua the Messiah only did what his Father told him to do, yet, he shared being human with us.

Paul speaks in his letters to Rome and Corinth and tells the people that soon they will crush the idols and pagan deities under their feet. The people are now free and engrafted into Messiah Yeshua. "The God of peace will soon crush Satan under your feet. The grace of our Lord Jesus Christ be with you" (Romans 16:20, ESV). Paul is telling them that they will have no need to worship in a pagan way. Paul was not telling them that they would soon be free of a sinful society or evil men. We know that today the adversary is wreaking havoc across the world. There is violence, drugs, sex trafficking, and unrest among the nations. In Paul's letters, The Satan or adversary he refers to is the idols that the people in Rome and Corinth had been worshipping. The Book of Peter gives a similar statement concerning issues that may at first seem to be speaking about the devil but are issues of the heart among God's people. "For out of the heart come evil thoughts, murder, adultery, sexual immorality, theft, false witness, slander" (Matthew 15:19, ESV).

Likewise, in I Peter, we are warned to stay alert, "Be sober, be vigilant; because your adversary the devil, as a roaring lion, walketh about, seeking whom he may devour" (I Peter 5:8, KJV). This passage is often quoted concerning the adversary. However, this chapter, when read in full, gives more context to the meaning of adversary. Peter is instructing elders, leadership, and the younger underneath these appointed positions of authority in the congregation. Peter names several temptations that could lead the overseers to stumble if they were not careful. He warns of being heavy-handed, compulsive, and longing to profit from preaching the Good News of Messiah Yeshua. The passage seems to imply that our flesh nature and temptations may rear their ugly head and roar like a lion:

> So I exhort the elders among you, as a fellow elder and a witness of the sufferings of Christ, as well as a partaker in the glory that is going to be revealed: shepherd the flock of God that is among you, exercising oversight, not under compulsion, but willingly, as God would have you; not for shameful gain, but eagerly; not domineering over those in your charge, but being examples to the flock. And when the chief Shepherd appears, you will receive the unfading crown of glory. Likewise, you who are younger, be subject to the elders. Clothe yourselves, all of you, with humility

toward one another, for "God opposes the proud but gives grace to the humble."

–I Peter 5:1-5, ESV

Directly after this first section directed at the leadership, Peter continues with a warning against those in positions of power to guard against their flesh nature that may erupt if they do not walk in a spirit of humility. Continuing with I Peter:

> Humble yourselves, therefore, under the mighty hand of God so that at the proper time he may exalt you, casting all your anxieties on him, because he cares for you. Be sober-minded; be watchful. Your adversary the devil prowls around like a roaring lion, seeking someone to devour. Resist him, firm in your faith, knowing that the same kinds of suffering are being experienced by your brotherhood throughout the world.

–I Peter 5:6-9, ESV

Peter informs the assembly that this suffering and testing is happening to the Body of Messiah throughout the world. They are not alone. He tells them to resist the adversary and be humble.

Knowing who our enemies are and how to defeat our enemies is necessary, especially when they are the person looking back at us in the mirror. One song sung often in children's church is titled *Enemy's Camp*. The song, written by

Lindell Cooley, showcases a story concerning David. The chorus states that the adversary is defeated and Satan is under our feet. The song refers to a passage from I Samuel. David and his men find that the Amalekites had invaded Ziklag, burned it, and taken their women and children captive. David's men were so troubled that they were ready to stone him. However, David recovers everything the enemy took from him in Ziklag. During this horrific time, David encouraged himself in Adonai:

> And David inquired of the LORD, "Shall I pursue after this band? Shall I overtake them?" He answered him, "Pursue, for you shall surely overtake and shall surely rescue."
>
> –I Samuel 30:8, ESV

David used wisdom. He asked the Lord if he should pursue the troops and go and retrieve his belongings. David did not proudly declare, "I am going to the enemy's camp, and Satan, you are a liar and a thief, and I am taking back what's mine." David, instead, sought the Father and asked Him if he should pursue the enemy and recover their belongings. David remained steadfast. The enemy he defeated was not Satan but the Amalekites.

Chapter 7

THE LITTLE GODS

PART 1

Once when my husband and I were house shopping, we went to look at a lovely home we saw online. The house had been vacant for a few years, and we were surprised, considering the acreage, location, and photos. When we arrived, we loved the house's landscape and outward appearance. The realtor gave us the home's history. The house had been empty for a long while. In the great room, there was a vaulted ceiling, and in the center of the room, a raised stage area. The realtor said, "Oh, yeah, I think they used to have bands they paid to come and entertain here. Behind the stage were a fireplace and bar area. We surmised the many updates needed, as the house was quite outdated. Besides that, we both felt a sense of uneasiness. A heaviness settled on us and an eerie feeling. I looked at my husband and said, "I don't feel at peace here." He said he did not either. We walked towards the bedrooms, and one bedroom had held squatters. The room had been vandalized, with walls filled with graffiti, curse words, obscene drawings, and drug paraphernalia scattered on the floor. The realtor apologized and said the owners had moved out of state; this was his first showing. More than the others, this bedroom seemed thick with deep darkness and some type of lingering spirit. (In *Book II, Spirits Unveiled*, I'll share more on spirits.) Although the realtor assured us the house was now secured, and no squatters had been in it for a good year, we could still feel something horrible in that house.

We are tents. We are houses. The apostle Paul states, "Or don't you know that your body is a temple of the Holy Spirit who is in you, whom you have from God, and that you are not your own? For you were bought with a price. Therefore, glorify God in your body" (I Corinthians 9:19-20, TLV). Although this verse is not meant to be taken singular as Paul was referring to the whole assembly, we too, are to be holy and set apart. A house left unattended or used for darkness has a different feel than one that is new and fresh and where the Holy Spirit is welcome. Our bodies are said to be where the Holy Spirit dwells and must be attended to. When a house is empty of the Holy Spirit and unattended, it can become polluted.

Spiritual leprosy can affect a house with uncleanness. Mentioned in the Book of Leviticus, there is an interesting story concerning a type of leprosy that the Holy One might "mark" in a person's house:

> *Adonai* spoke to Moses and to Aaron, saying: "Suppose you have come into the land of Canaan, which I give to you

for a possession, and I put a mark of *tza'arat* (leprosy) in a house in the land you possess. Then the one who owns the house should come and tell the *kohen*, saying: 'Something like a mark has appeared in my house.'"

–Leviticus 14:33-35, TLV

During the time of Moses, the priest would come to inspect a home that had the condition mentioned in Leviticus. Sometimes the houses had to be torn down due to mold or other issues. Our houses can become toxic:

The priest must order that the house be cleared before he enters it to examine the mildew, so that nothing in the house will become unclean. After this, the priest shall go in to inspect the house. He is to examine the house, and if the mildew on the walls consists of green or red depressions that appear to be beneath the surface of the wall, the priest shall go outside the doorway of the house and close it up for seven days.

–Leviticus 14:36-38, BSB

This disrepair and leprosy can happen today in our fleshly bodies. Many today may mock demons and darkness, while others seek after it with vigor, unaware that dabbling in darkness always leads to death of the spirit and possibly the body.

Also, there is a reason why the Holy One forbids witchcraft and necromancy. When Adam and Eve (*Chavah*) ate from the tree of knowledge of good and evil, they were made aware of things they had not experienced before eating. Adam and Chavah had always been naked, but now they were aware they were naked. They had been listening to the Voice of the Holy One, but now they were hiding from Him. After eating from the tree of knowledge of good and evil, they were not allowed back into the garden. They were aware of both good and evil, order and disorder. There was a hidden realm exposed that they now would not be given access to unveil. Dabbling in the occult has become popular today. Now that we have the World Wide Web and Google at our fingertips, we can read up on witchcraft, incantations, curses, crystals, herbs, and multiple ways to cast spells; but the Bible warns against this. "You must not allow a sorceress to live" (Exodus 22:18, BSB). We must seek life and not death. Heightened knowledge, as with Adam and Chavah, can lead to destruction of the spirit and/or body.

As the world becomes older, knowledge is increasing just as the Bible predicted it would. "Many will run back and forth, and knowledge will increase'" (Daniel 12:4, TLV). Knowledge has indeed increased, but knowledge without wisdom and understanding is simply knowledge. People can have knowledge of how a car operates, but if they have never driven a car and have attempted to drive without training, driving could be dangerous. Today many have left Christianity for New Age, Wiccan religions, and Satanism, among others. They are searching to fill their empty houses, but this search for knowledge can be counterfeit and dangerous. Any reasonable person who knows the difference between fool's gold and real gold would never trade the real thing for a worthless stone. Sometimes when the Bible is taught and read with ignorance, it is similar to fool's gold. Even the words good and evil and light and darkness need enlightening in Hebraic terms. *Abarim Publications*, who I quote often, has a definition concerning light and darkness that explains the contrast of each clearly:

> The prophet Isaiah says it this way: "I am YHWH, and *there is no other*! I am the One forming light (אור, *'or*) and the One creating darkness, making שלום (*shalom*, wholeness) and ער (*ra'*, evil, = brokenness, the absence of wholeness). I am YHWH who does all these" (Isaiah 45:7). Despite rumors to the contrary, darkness is not the opposite of light but the absence of it. Darkness is the absence of light and not the presence of something else. Likewise, cold is the absence of heat, not the presence of something else. Ignorance is the absence of wisdom, not the presence of something else. Chaos is the absence of order, not the presence of something else. [10]

Therefore, darkness is the absence of light. The light shines brighter in the darkness. If one were to light a candle in a pitch-black room, the light would shine, illuminating the room. David

---

[10] satan | The amazing name satan: meaning and etymology (abarim-publications.com)

describes the Holy One as dwelling in thick darkness:

> He made darkness His cover, His *sukkah* all around
> Him—dark waters, thick clouds.
>
> —Psalm 18:12, TLV

Because of the darkness, humans cannot view the fullness of the Holy One or all His glory, as this would result in sudden death. Also, Exodus 20 confirms that Adonai dwells in darkness:

> And Moses said to the people, "Do not fear; for God has
> come to test you, and that His fear may be before you, so
> that you may not sin." So the people stood afar off, but
> Moses drew near the thick darkness where God *was*.
>
> —Exodus 20:20, NKJ

In Exodus 33, Moses informs the Holy One that he longs to see His glory. "Please reveal your glory to me," Moses pleads. God answers Moses and states that no one could live if He revealed His Face:

> But He said, "You cannot see My face; for no man shall see
> Me, and live." And the Lord said, "Here is a place by Me,
> and you shall stand on the rock. So it shall be, while My
> glory passes by, that I will put you in the cleft of the rock,
> and will cover you with My hand while I pass by. Then I
> will take away My hand, and you shall see My back; but
> My face shall not be seen.
>
> —Exodus 33:20-23, NKJ

The Holy One may reside in thick darkness at times, but He is a God that speaks, possesses emotions, and is all-knowing. The Holy One has no beginning or ending—He exists; He just is.

Do other gods exist? Different groups of people worship a variety of different gods. Do other gods exist? Did ancient societies start by blindly guessing concerning a god with primitive concepts? Stories were passed down concerning the earth, which became the "Mother" earth. The sun, the moon, the stars, storms, and creatures of all kinds became gods or had a superior god who controlled them. The first gods were fundamental, but over time, they became giants called Titan's. If "little gods" such as these various and primitive gods exist, who are they compared to the God of Abraham, Isaac, and Jacob? The Torah states that we should have no other gods before Adonai. "You shall have no other gods before Me" (Exodus 20:3, TLV). If there were no other gods in existence, why would we be warned? The warning relates to further references to "little" gods. After the triumph of the Israelites through the Reed or Red Sea, Miriam and Moses sang a song. One of the lyrics states, "Who is like You, *Adonai*, among the gods?" (Exodus 15:11, TLV). Sadly, after Adonai wreaks havoc on Pharoah, parts the Reed Sea, and releases them from slavery, they ask Aaron to make a golden calf for them to worship—a little god. In anger, Moses sees their idolatry and throws the commandments, breaking them.

Other men like Moses tried to cleanse God's people from idolatry, "little gods." In II Kings 23, Josiah, King of Judah, did away with the idolatrous priests ordained by the kings of Judah who had burned incense to Baal and the whole host of heaven. There would be no other gods before Adonai during his reign. Josiah took the Asherah poles and burned them in the Kidron valley. Curiously, Kidron means "Very black, full of darkness." [11] He burned the Asherah pole to powder like Moses ground the golden calf to powder when he came down the mountain and saw the people worshipping it. Josiah removed the shrines and the areas for the male prostitutes. He removed so many idols and high places that the whole chapter of II Kings 23 is filled with this king's cleansing of the land:

> He also desecrated Topheth in the Valley of Ben-hinnom so that no one could sacrifice his son or daughter in the fire to Molech. And he removed from the entrance to the house of the LORD the horses that the kings of Judah had dedicated to the sun. They were in the court near the chamber of an official named Nathan-melech. And Josiah burned up the chariots of the sun. He pulled down the altars that the kings of Judah had set up on the roof near the upper chamber of Ahaz, and the altars that Manasseh had set up in the two courtyards of the house of the LORD. The king pulverized them there and

---

[11] Kidron | The amazing name Kidron: meaning and etymology (abarim-publications.com)

threw their dust into the Kidron Valley.

–II Kings 23:10-12, BSB

Josiah honored the Holy One, destroyed the little gods, and began cleansing the land.

Unlike righteous Josiah, Pharaoh believed he was a god and that he created the Nile, but the Holy One told Pharaoh plainly that although he thought he was a god, he was just a man:

> "Behold, I am against you, Pharaoh king of Egypt, The great monster that lies in the midst of his canals, That has said, 'My Nile is mine, and I myself have made *it*.'""

–Ezekiel 29:3, ASV

The Israelites were warned in the Commandments not to follow the gods of the people around them, such as Astarte, Chemosh, and Dagon. Multiple gods are mentioned in the Bible, but Ba'al is mentioned more than all the other gods. Ba'al is a title given to the god *Hadad*. Ba'al was the god of thunderstorms and rain. Was Ba'al a little god or a figment of the people's imagination? In I Kings 18, Elijah has a showdown between the god Ba'al and the Holy One. The prophets of Ba'al prepared a bull and laid it on the altar but did not light a fire. They called on the name of Ba'al from morning until noon, shouting, "O Baal, answer us!" No one answered. They leaped around the altar and cut themselves, and cried out, but no response was heard from Ba'al. At the time of the evening sacrifice, Elijah approached the altar and said a humble prayer to the God of Abraham, Isaac, and Jacob:

> Answer me, O LORD! Answer me, so that this people will know that You, the LORD, are God, and that You have turned their hearts back again. "Then the fire of the LORD fell and consumed the sacrifice, the wood, the stones, and the dust, and it licked up the water in the trench. When all the people saw this, they fell facedown and said, "The LORD, He is God! The LORD, He is God!"'
>
> —I Kings 18:37-39, BSB

Afterward, the prophet Elijah commands all the prophets of Ba'al to be slaughtered in the Kidron Valley—very dark and full of blackness.

Further, David proclaimed that there are no gods like Adonai. "There is none like You among the gods, my Lord, there are no deeds like Yours" (Psalm 86:8, TLV). "For great is *Adonai*, and greatly to be praised. He is to be feared above all gods. For all the gods of the peoples are idols, but *Adonai* made the heavens. (Psalm 96:4, TLV). Since the beginning of time, people have worshipped many gods. On *Psychology Today* website, in his article *Why Do Humans Keep Inventing Gods to Worship?* Gary Wenk, Ph.D., places a number on the deities worshipped:

> Anthropologists estimate that at least 18,000 different gods, goddesses, and various animals or objects have been worshipped by humans since our species first appeared.

Today, it is estimated that more than 80 percent of the global population considers themselves religious or spiritual in some form. [12]

Wenk gives an example of how the god Ra disappeared after a long run of converts. Many gods were worshipped for lengthy periods and then essentially disappeared from the historical record. Ra was worshipped by many different cultures for thousands of years before disappearing completely.

---

[12] Why Do Humans Keep Inventing Gods to Worship? | Psychology Today

Chapter 7

THE LITTLE GODS

PART 2

Unlike the vast worship of different gods, the top four or five religions of the world are monotheistic. Today there are five main religions: Christianity, Judaism, Islam, Buddhism, and Hinduism. According to general statistics, a person born in Pakistan would likely be a Muslim as over 97% of the people living there are Muslim. A person born in India would likely be Hindu as over 80% of the population is Hindu. What about America? Recent polls suggest approximately 70% of Americans are Christians:

> According to the Pew Research Center's studies, Islam is the fastest-growing religion in the world. Forecasts suggest that in the second half of the 21st century, Muslims will replace Christians as the world's largest religious group. The global Muslim population is projected to increase from 1.8 billion to 3 billion from 2015 to 2060.[13]

---

[13] Reasons Why Muslims Are The World's Fastest-growing Religious Group

Again, Muslims of the Islamic faith are monotheistic. They, too, believe in the God of Abraham. They believe their god is the ruler and creator of the universe. Allah is a personal name for the god of Islam. *Allah* in Arabic means one true God, but the characteristics of their god and the God of the Jews is vastly different.

Although the Muslim population is growing, Hebrew Christianity is rapidly spreading as well. According to the *Messianic Jewish Alliance of America,* "There are now tens of thousands of Messianic Jews in the United States alone; some estimate as many as 1.2 million. Messianic synagogues are springing up in almost every major city across the U.S., and Messianic Judaism is quickly growing in other nations throughout North and South America, Europe, Oceania, and the former Soviet republics." [14]

Do Hindus believe in one god? Contrary to widespread misconceptions, Hindus worship one supreme being called by many different names. The Vedas are the most ancient Hindu hymns, prayers, philosophy, and writings on guidance. Much of the Vedas is read with great honor to the Creator of all the universe:

> In the Vedas, we find nowhere any such mention which may be concluded to show that Hinduism believes in more

---

- WorldAtlas
[14] Messianic Movement | MJAA Messianic Jewish Alliance of America

Gods than one. Vedas, Upanishads (Hindu sacred treatises) and all other authorized scriptures clearly speak of One God and the only God that permeates the universe. He is the Supreme Being – Yajurveda (XLI) says," By one supreme Ruler is the universe pervaded. Even every world in the whole circle of nature, He is the True God... For Him, O Man, covet not unjustly the wealth of any creature existing. Renounce all that is unjust and enjoy pure delight, true spiritual happiness." [15]

Therefore, in fact, Hindus all worship one supreme being by different names. Just as Christians might call God by the title God, Lord, Jehovah, or the God of Abraham, Isaac, and Jacob, in Messianic congregations, they may call Him Adonai, HaShem, Yahweh, etc. However, Hinduism is drastically different than the God of Abraham, Isaac, and Jacob.

Those raised to honor their deities and invoke their god bring their god gifts, prayers, and obedience. In Japan, Buddhism reigns supreme. They have what is called *Four Noble Truths*. Buddha was a man who lived through great wealth and traded it for poverty and suffering and then found balance. His writings ministered to many as he gained wisdom from what he experienced. According to Buddhists' noble truths, a person is responsible for suffering due to thoughts that give birth to greed, hatred, and delusion and contribute to suffering. One quote from

---

[15] Do Hindus Believe in More Gods than One? by R. K. Lahri (boloji.com)

this belief says, "Greed is always looking for more and never thinking enough is enough."

They also live by five moral precepts, which prohibit:

1. Abstain from killing

2. Abstain from stealing

3. Abstain from sexual misconduct

4. Abstain from lying

5. Abstain from the use of intoxicating substances that cause inattention [16]

Many of these five moral precepts mimic the Ten Sayings or Ten Commandments. The Christian Messiah, Yeshua, Jesus, said, "I am the way, the truth, and the life. No one comes to the Father except through Me" (John 14:6, NKJV). Regardless of the different religions aforementioned or their gods, Yeshua said He was the way to life and life more abundantly. No one can come to the Father, the Holy One, except through Him. The Messiah said He was the Word (Torah/ Tree of Life) made flesh. Applying this knowledge, we must seek after the Messiah's words and actions and mimic them. According to John, the Messiah Yeshua was the Word made flesh, and according to the prophets, His Torah/commandments lead us in the way of righteousness, reveal the truth, and bring true life. Psalm 119 gives more understanding of the way, the truth, and the life:

---

[16] The 5 Precepts: Buddhism and Morality | Buddho.org

Blessed are those whose way is blameless, who walk in the Law {Torah} of the LORD. Blessed are those who keep His testimonies and seek Him with all their heart. They do no iniquity; they walk in His ways.

–Psalms 119:1-3, BSB

The unfolding of Your words gives light; it informs the simple.

–Psalm 119;130, BSB

Your word is a lamp to my feet and a light to my path.

–Psalm 119:105, BSB

Once again, Jesus spoke to the people and said, "I am the light of the world. Whoever follows Me will never walk in the darkness, but will have the light of life."

–John 8:12, BSB

In Him was life, and that life was the light of men.

–John 1:4, BSB

Many people shall come and say, "Come, and let us go up to the mountain of the Lord, To the house of the God of Jacob; He will teach us His ways, And we shall walk in His paths." For out of Zion shall go forth the law {Torah}, And the word of the Lord from Jerusalem.

–Isaiah 2:3, NKJ

Additionally, in I Thessalonians 5, Paul discusses the Day of the Lord and how the Messiah will return like a thief in the night which is an idiom for the Feast of Trumpets. He tells those who walk in the way that they are of the light:

> But you, brothers, are not in the darkness so that this day should overtake you like a thief. For you are all sons of the light and sons of the day; we do not belong to the night or to the darkness.
>
> —I Thessalonians 5:4-5, BSB

In John, when the Messiah said that no man could come to the Father except through Him, He meant this. Yeshua openly states that He is the Door for the sheep. In Egypt, the Israelites had to slay a lamb and place its blood on their doorposts so the death angel would bypass their dwelling places. This represents Yeshua, the Lamb of God who takes away the sins of the world.

The Egyptians awoke to the death of their firstborn sons, and God's people heard their wailing and knew the blood had spared their households from death. There is power in the blood of Yeshua. The Israelites had been living in a culture with many gods. A people coming out of Egypt needed to see and understand that the gods of Egypt were worthless compared to Adonai. The gods and goddesses of Ancient Egypt were an integral part of the people's everyday lives, and the Israelites spent over 400 years in this environment. The Egyptians had thousands of deities. The Biblical story of the exodus is about

Elohim having a showdown against all the Egyptian gods. The magicians of Egypt, by their magic arts, made the water turn to blood just as Aaron, they brought frogs up onto the land of Egypt just as Aaron, but the gnats they could not reproduce. Their magicians told Pharaoh, "This is the Finger of God." Yes, even sorcerers knew this power was from the heavens. At the end of the event, every god the Egyptians worshipped, from the god of locust, Senehem, to the god of flies, Uatchit, was sent to destroy the people who worshipped them. The Holy One sent thousands of locusts that were said to blot out the sun (Ra). He sent darkness for three days, but the children of Israel had light in Goshen, where they resided. Not only do we hear of these miracles, but the death of the firstborn of Egypt was also a darkness that could be seen and felt. The God of the Hebrews mocked the little gods of Egypt by showcasing His power over all creation.

Like the Egyptians, the ancient Greeks believed in many deities and spirits. Because knowledge of the world was limited in antiquity, the Ancients attributed natural phenomena to higher powers. Gods and goddesses could be found everywhere and defined the lives of the people. Zeus (Jupiter, in Roman mythology) was said to be the king of all the gods and father to many. Hera (Juno) was the queen of the gods. The Greek gods even declared war on each other.

In the days of the apostles, so many gods were worshipped

that Paul addressed this issue while visiting Mars Hill. When the Apostle Paul visited Athens, there were thousands of gods in idol structure. According to the Colson Center, "Athens had a population of 10,000 people—and 30,000 pagan statues. So many idols choked the landscape because its citizens were afraid to provoke the gods to wrath by inadvertently overlooking them."[17] Mars Hill is the Roman name for a hill in Athens, Greece, rising over 370 feet above the land below. Mars Hill served as the meeting place for the highest court in Greece for civil, criminal, and religious matters. Mars Hill is the place Paul stood. Imagine the scene as he addressed the people:

> So Paul stood in the middle of the Aereopagus and said, "Men of Athens, I see that in all ways you are very religious. For while I was passing through and observing the objects of your worship, I even found an altar with this inscription: 'To an Unknown God.' Therefore what you worship without knowing, this I proclaim to you. The God who made the world and all things in it, since He is Lord of heaven and earth, does not live in temples made by hands. Nor is He served by human hands, as if He needed anything, since He Himself gives to everyone life and breath and all things. From one He made every nation of men to live on the face of the earth, having set appointed times and the boundaries of their territory. They were to

---

[17] Ascending Mars Hill - Breakpoint

search for Him, and perhaps grope around for Him and find Him. Yet He is not far from each one of us, for 'In Him we live and move and have our being.' As some of your own poets have said, 'For we also are His offspring.' Since we are His offspring, we ought not to suppose the Deity is like gold or silver or stone, an engraved image of human art and imagination. Although God overlooked the periods of ignorance, now He commands everyone everywhere to repent. For He has set a day on which He will judge the world in righteousness, through a Man whom He has appointed. He has brought forth evidence of this to all men, by raising Him from the dead."

–Acts 17:22-31, TLV

Paul was explaining to the people of Athens that at one time, due to ignorance, the Holy One had overlooked man's ways, but He would not any longer. Now the Holy One was desiring repentance from their worship of other gods. Paul was addressing the idolatry of these Greek gods and goddesses. The authors of the Bible wrote from the societies around them. The Bible lists the names of over 50 gods. Some of these gods were more popular than others, such as Dagon, Baal, Ashtoreth, Chemosh, Diana, El, and Zeus. Paul addressed the men at Athens and expressed that he had observed that they were very "religious" concerning their multiple gods, but the word religious is not accurate. The word religious did not exist at the time of this writing. Paul said they were *daimonesterous*. Strong's Greek 1174 defines very religious as δεισιδαιμονεστέρους (*daimonesterous*). [18] This comes from the root *daimon*-- the exact root from which we get the word demon. Paul was expressing that the men at Athens were very aware of what they were doing and the idolatry that encased them, and he declared that the Holy One was no longer going to tolerate such demonic behavior.

To further the ideas of little gods, the first commandment states we are to have no other gods before Adonai. This is disobedience. In Hebrew thought, evil is something that is not working in divine order or the order the Creator created for divine order to function. One example is a potter who made a pitcher to hold water but accidentally dropped it, breaking it into pieces. The pitcher can no longer do what it was created to do. Humans were created by the Creator of all the earth. They were given instructions for fulfilling their purposes, but what happens when those instructions are thrown out in disregard? Society is left to make its own gods and its own governments. Instead of eating from the Tree of Life and living in peace, chaos and disorder occur. The Tree of Life is the Torah/commandments. King David, a prototype of Yeshua Messiah, explains that these instructions are worth more than gold:

---

[18] Acts 17:22 Parallel: Then Paul stood in the midst of Mars' hill, and said, Ye men of Athens, I perceive that in all things ye are too superstitious. (biblehub.com)

Oh, how I love Your law (Torah)! It *is* my meditation all the day. You, through Your commandments, make me wiser than my enemies; For they *are* ever with me. I have more understanding than all my teachers, For Your testimonies *are* my meditation. I understand more than the ancients because I keep Your precepts. I have restrained my feet from every evil way, That I may keep Your word. I have not departed from Your judgments, For You Yourself have taught me. How sweet are Your words to my taste, *Sweeter* than honey to my mouth! Through Your precepts I get understanding; Therefore I hate every false way.

–Psalm 119:97-104, NKJ

When we disobey Adonai's instructions and become rebellious, we can open dangerous doors. Just as the house mentioned at the beginning of this chapter looked good on the outside, the inside was unlivable. When we allow drugs, pornography, drunkenness, and darkness into our temples where the Holy Spirit is to dwell, we leave ourselves open for demonic possession or oppression. We become like Pharaohs thinking we are gods. In Matthew 15, Yeshua explains the matter, and it has nothing to do with the serpent in the Garden or a fallen angel; it has all to do with the condition of our hearts:

For out of the heart come evil thoughts, murder, adultery, sexual immorality, theft, false testimony, and slander.

These are what defile a man. . .

–Matthew 15:119-20, BSB

As for the Greeks, their gods had instructions that were perverted, and the Greeks loved to explore their thoughts concerning each god with great pomp. Greece Tours website offers a plethora of information concerning Greece, Delphi, Sparta, Olympia, and Athens and multiple Christian blogs. One article of interest features the Apostle Paul at Mar's Hill and is titled *Sacred Mars Hill (Areopagus) the One and Only:*

> We know from history that the Epicurean philosophers generally believed that God existed but that He was not interested or involved with humanity and that the main purpose of life was a pleasure. On the other hand, the Stoic philosophers had the worldview that "God was the world's soul" and that the goal of life was "to rise above all things" so that one showed no emotional response to either pain or pleasure. These groups and others with their dramatically opposing worldviews loved to discuss and debate philosophy and religion. Intrigued by what they considered Paul's "babblings" about the resurrection of Christ, they brought him to the Areopagus where the Athenians and foreigners "spent their time in nothing else but to tell or hear some new thing."[19]

---

[19] Sacred Mars Hill (Areopagus)! The(1) one and only! (bestgreecetours.com)

The Apostle Paul was not impressed by their babbling or their many little gods adorning Mars Hill. He was speaking as the Holy Spirit led him. But the men of Athens were not the only men caught up in idols and egos. The prophets give multiple explanations for the idolatry of their days and the little gods placed in leadership.

What causes sin and wars in nations? The prophets express that the rulers of the nation play a significant role in the situation:

> O My people! Those who lead you cause *you* to err and destroy the way of your paths.
>
> –Isaiah 3:12, NKJ

Jeremiah states that the people in power love the corruption:

> The prophets prophesy falsely, And the priests rule by their *own* power; And My people love *to have it* so. But what will you do in the end?"
>
> –Jeremiah 5:31, NKJ

The Book of Proverbs has multiple verses concerning unrighteous leadership:

> Like a roaring lion or a charging bear is a wicked ruler over a helpless people.
>
> –Proverbs 28:15, BSB

When the righteous flourish, the people rejoice, but when the wicked rule, the people groan.

> −Proverbs 29:2, BSB

Today's little gods are mostly the same as Israel's but with different titles. Of late, many of the gods of Egypt and Greece are making a comeback. Hermes, god of commerce, presides over the Grand Central Terminal in New York City. Rockefeller Center hosts Prometheus, a titan god of fire, and Atlas, upholding the cosmos. Athena Parthenos stands in the lobby of the Metropolitan Museum of Art. The Parthenon is not just in Centennial Park. A full-scale replica of the original Parthenon in Athens stands proudly in Nashville, Tennessee. However, the prophets and mainly Jeremiah express that idols are worthless and breathless and will one day perish:

> Every man is senseless and devoid of knowledge; every goldsmith is put to shame by his idols. For his molten images are a fraud, and there is no breath in them. They are worthless, a work to be mocked. In the time of their punishment they will perish.
>
> −Jeremiah 51:17-18, BSB

The Greek gods were known for forcing women into performing sexual acts. Older males sought younger males for sex, and there were both male and female prostitutes. In ancient Semitic religions, Asherah was worshiped through ritual sex. The worshipers participated in sex to cause the god Ba'al and

Asherah to join together. These sexual acts were expressed in obscene public prostitution. Today, everywhere we look, there is a form of sexual enticement. One cannot turn on the television without sexually explicit situations. Even the commercials are perverse. *CBS Family* has a series called *The Good Wife*, rated 14. Children 14 years of age and older can watch this according to their standards.

The television show depicts sexual scenes. Orgasms. Men and women in dog collars with chains and sex toys. Conversations about oral sex between men and women, men and men, and women and women. Also, sexual scenes with a college-aged girl seducing a 14-year-old boy. And this example is mild today. Open a computer browser, and sex or explicit photos that enhance areas of the body are paraded about boldly. Sex sells. Sex entices. In an interview, the serial killer Jeffrey Dahmer was asked how he ended up mutilating his victims, having sex with their corpses, and eating their flesh. I paraphrase his response, "I became desensitized and began to become obsessed with pornography." In the last interview given to Ted Bundy, he expressed that he became exposed to violent pornography at an early age. The wages of sin lead to death. Before the flood, the Holy One was saddened and grieved that He had created man:

> Then *Adonai* saw that the wickedness of humankind was great on the earth and that every inclination of the thoughts of their heart was only evil all the

time. So *Adonai* regretted that He made humankind on the earth, and His heart was deeply pained. So *Adonai* said, "I will wipe out humankind, whom I have created, from the face of the ground, from humankind to livestock, crawling things and the flying creatures of the sky, because I regret that I made them.

–Genesis 6:5-7, TLV

In Genesis 6, the Holy One does not place the blame on Satan for the wickedness that has filled the earth but instead expounds on the thoughts of men's hearts. The Book of Jasher, referred to in Joshua 10:13, and II Samuel 1:18 expounds on the main issue. According to Jasher, it was not men sleeping with angels but wicked judges and rulers that went to the daughters of men and took their wives by force from their husbands according to their choice. These types of men mentioned in the Book of Jasher acted as "little gods" and thought the Holy One would look away, but instead, He sent a deluge. In fact, the answer concerning little gods can be found in the first Book of the Bible, Genesis/Bereshit. It is recorded that we were created in the image of the Holy One and that we were to rule over the earth. Not like the Pharaoh with harsh taskmasters, but in divine order. "Be fruitful and multiply, fill the land, and conquer it. Rule over the fish of the sea, the flying creatures of the sky, and over every animal that crawls on the land" (Genesis 1:28, TLV). But instead, man began to worship the sun, moon, stars, and creatures instead of the Creator. Man became filled with pride. The apostle Paul explains that all men are without excuse when it comes to acknowledging the Creator and His Glory, and explains that since the beginning of time, men knew God:

> His (the Holy One's) invisible attributes—His eternal power and His divine nature—have been clearly seen ever since the creation of the world, being understood through the things that have been made. So people are without excuse— for even though they knew God, they did not glorify Him as God or give Him thanks. Instead, their thinking became futile, and their senseless hearts were made dark. Claiming to be wise, they became fools. They exchanged the glory of the immortal God for an image in the form of mortal man and birds and four-footed beasts and creeping things.
>
> —Romans 1:20-23, TLV

Paul went on to explain how these men who did not see fit to recognize God as the Creator of all things were given over to a corrupt mind. Instead of the mind of Yeshua, they became like the house my husband, and I toured. They became consumed with death and the things associated with death. The little gods of lust, drunkenness, drugs, and witchcraft took over their temples or houses.

In ancient times, even those ignorant of the God of the Hebrews were aware that something greater than them created thunder, lightning, rain showers, and snow and caused the seasons to change. Today we have put men on the moon. We can see and speak with people across the globe on our handheld phones. We are far advanced in medicine, technology, and science. Perhaps we have made ourselves gods. Jacob told his sons in Genesis 35 to put away their little gods. May we do as Jacob and prepare an altar in our hearts and homes unto the one and only God, Adonai:

> So Jacob said to his household and to everyone who was with him, "Get rid of the foreign gods that are among you. Cleanse yourselves and change your clothes. Now let's get up and go up to Beth-El so that I can make an altar there to God, who answered me in the day of my distress, and has been with me in the way that I have gone."'
>
> –Genesis 35:2-3, TLV

Chapter 8

THE EVIL INCLINATION

When studying the adversary from the beginning to the end of the Bible, one can find multiple clues. The serpent was right there in the garden. The Father was not unaware. There is no indication that this serpent snuck in and tempted Eve (*Chavah*), and the Holy One was oblivious. All things were created by Him and for His purpose:

> For by him all things were created, in heaven and on earth, visible and invisible, whether thrones or dominions or rulers or authorities—all things were created through him and for him.
>
> –Colossians 1:16, ESV

Unlike Adonai, Satan is not omnipresent, omnipotent, or omniscient as mentioned earlier in chapter 3. Often, the scriptures used to describe Satan have not been thoroughly scrutinized. One popular book used to describe Satan or the Devil is the Book of Job. There is no record of Job or his friends talking to Satan or cursing him. At the closing of Job, we learn that Job prayed for his friends, who then repented, and then the

Holy One restored Job's health and family. James, the brother of Yeshua, used Job and the prophets as an example when suffering:

> As an example of suffering and patience, brothers, take the prophets who spoke in the name of the Lord. Behold, we consider those blessed who remained steadfast. You have heard of the steadfastness of Job, and you have seen the purpose of the Lord, how the Lord is compassionate and merciful.
>
> –James 5:10-11, ESV

Ha-Satan (the Accuser) did not point Job out to Adonai when he was walking the earth. Adonai said, "Have you considered my servant Job?" (Job 1:8, KJV). God allowed the adversary to do what he wished, but he was to spare Job's life: "And the Father said unto Satan, Behold all that he (Job) hath is in thy power, only upon himself put not forth thine hand" (Job 1:12, KJV). Job did not declare Satan was under his feet as many in Christianity do. Job, in humility, said, "Naked I came from my mother's womb, and naked shall I return. The LORD gave, and the LORD has taken away; blessed be the name of the LORD." (Job 1:21, ESV). Job blessed the name of the Lord instead of cursing ha-Satan. James 4, concerning steadfastness during adversity, rings true throughout the Book of Job.

One sacred cow or unreasonable teaching thought to be immune from criticism implies that Job opened a door and tore a place in the hedge of protection God had placed around him. The passage used to promote this church dogma suggests Job allowed a spirit of fear to come in: "For the thing that I fear comes upon me, and what I dread befalls me" (Job 3: 25, ESV). This doctrine implies that Job, by letting fear in, made a gap in the hedge of protection. A closer look while reviewing the whole chapter suggests Job is talking about death:

> Why is light given to him who is in misery, and life to the bitter in soul, who long for death, but it comes not, and dig for it more than for hidden treasures, who rejoice exceedingly and are glad when they find the grave? Why is light given to a man whose way is hidden, whom God has hedged in? For my sighing comes instead of my bread, and my groaning's are poured out like water. For the thing that I fear comes upon me.

> –Job 3:20-25, ESV

The passage above states Job is still hedged in and protected. The context explains Job fears he will not die but will continue suffering horrifically. The verses imply Job was righteous and not a man of fear. "There was a man in the land of Uz whose name was Job, and that man was blameless and upright, one who feared God and turned away from evil" (Job 1:1, ESV). The Father, not Satan, allowed the adversity into Job's life:

> Then came to him all his brothers and sisters and all who had known him before, and ate bread with him in his

house. And they showed him sympathy and comforted him for all the evil that the LORD had brought upon him. And each of them gave him a piece of money and a ring of gold.

—Job 42:11, ESV

Although Job had flaws like all humans, fear was not what the passages in Job 3:20-25 were concerning. His fear was continuing to suffer horrifically with no end in sight.

Our thoughts can invoke fear and be a Satan or an adversarial voice in our heads. When Yeshua spoke of his death and suffering and resurrection, Peter said, no, it must not be, but how does Messiah answer him?

But He turned and said to Peter, "Get behind Me, Satan! You are a stumbling block to Me; for you are not setting your mind on God's purposes, but men's."

—Matthew 16:21, NASB

As we apply our Hebraic spectacles, we see the context in a different light. We know Peter was not a red-horned serpent. Peter was speaking through ignorance. Peter was speaking as an adversary who could not see that the Messiah had to suffer and die to fulfill all things.

Also, the apostle Paul uses the term Satan on several occasions. Paul addresses the Body of Believers in Corinth, and he gives needed correction:

> It is actually reported that there is sexual immorality among you, and of a kind that is not tolerated even among pagans, for a man has his father's wife. And you are arrogant! Ought you not rather to mourn? Let him who has done this be removed from among you.
>
> –I Corinthians 5:1-2, ESV

The apostle Paul continues to bring correction, but when taken out of context, his message to a man in the assembly who had fallen into sin might seem quite peculiar:

> You are to deliver this man to Satan for the destruction of the flesh, so that his spirit may be saved in the day of the Lord.
>
> –I Corinthians 5:5, ESV

Paul was teaching the Gospel of Messiah to a people who were used to multiple gods and goddesses. Temple prostitution and orgies were highly prevalent. Paul was reprimanding the person caught up in sexual sins publicly so that the others would understand this sexual behavior would not be tolerated. After the sinner was turned over to Satan, or the adversary, he would become repulsed by his flesh nature, seeking repentance. Sin is only pleasurable for a season, then it leads to death. The one caught in sexual sin would realize after a time that there was no freedom or life in this type of debauchery. And by removing the person from a loving Torah community, they, like Miriam, would be isolated and repent.

Everett Ferguson, distinguished author, teacher, and scholar, gives more insight as to what the culture was like in Corinth during the days of the apostles in her article *Cult Prostitution in the New Testament*:

> All kinds of immoralities were associated with the [Greco-Roman] gods. Not only was prostitution a recognized institution, but through the influence of the fertility cults of Asia Minor, Syria, and Phoenicia, it became a part of the religious rites at certain temples. Thus there were one thousand "sacred prostitutes" at the temple of Aphrodite at Corinth. [20]

Paul later explains that after the people are removed because of their sins, the one turned over to Satan (their flesh nature) should be restored with gentleness and love:

> Brothers, if anyone is caught in any transgression, you who are spiritual should restore him in a spirit of gentleness. Keep watch on yourself, lest you too be tempted.
>
> –Galatians 6:1, ESV

Again, this matter of turning one over to Satan had nothing to do with a fallen angel or cherub; it has to do with immorality and our flesh.

---

[20] https://biblicalstudies.org.uk/article_ephesus_baugh.html#1

In II Timothy, Paul speaks of an adversary who hindered the good news of the Messiah from going forth. This more than likely was Alexander:

> Alexander the coppersmith did me great harm; the Lord will repay him according to his deeds. Beware of him yourself, for he strongly opposed our message.
>
> –II Timothy 4:14-15, ESV

> Wherefore we would have come unto you, even I Paul, once and again; but Satan hindered us.
>
> –I Thessalonians 2:18, KJV

Paul said an adversary hindered him. Paul does not mean that a fallen angel hindered him, he means the Judaizers caused trouble. Hebrew is a phenomenological language. It expresses the way things appear, not the ways things actually are. The Holy One is still in control. Again, nowhere do we see the apostles or disciples screaming and yelling at Satan, commanding him to obey them, or saying he cannot cross their bloodline as many in the Body of Messiah are speaking through ignorance. The translation simply means adversary. Continuing with Messiah and His time in the wilderness brings further understanding to the conundrum. In Matthew 4, Yeshua, after fasting 40 days and nights, is tempted on all points:

> Then *Yeshua* was led by the *Ruach* into the wilderness to be tempted by the devil. After He had fasted for forty days

and forty nights, He was hungry.

–Matthew 4:1-2, TLV

The tempter came. There are multiple titles used for this adversary. He is called by several names, such as Satan, the accuser, the evil inclination, or the devil. However, these titles often suggest someone is acting as an adversary, and sometimes, as in the case of Peter, when Yeshua said, "get thee behind me Satan," we are the Satan. In Hebrew thought, Satan is the archetype of wickedness or acting in our beastly nature. The provoking to do or act in an evil manner is an alternative. It is a force within an individual rather than an influence from without. Every human being has two desires, one to do evil and the other to do good. Remember Cain and Abel, Esau, and Jacob. In most biblical stories, we read of one man with a stronger evil inclination and one with a righteous tendency. The Cherokee Indians have a parable called *Two Wolves* that explains this superbly:

> *An old Cherokee chief was teaching his grandson about life...*
>
> "A fight is going on inside me," he said to the boy.
> "It is a terrible fight and it is between two wolves.
>
> "One is evil – he is fear, anger, envy, sorrow, regret, greed, arrogance, self-pity, guilt, resentment, inferiority, lies, false pride, superiority, self-doubt, and ego.

"The other is good – he is joy, peace, love, hope, serenity, humility, kindness, benevolence, empathy, generosity, truth, compassion, and faith.

"This same fight is going on inside you – and inside every other person, too."

The grandson thought about it for a minute and then asked his grandfather,
"Which wolf will win?"

The old chief simply replied,
"The one you feed." [21]

--Author Unknown.

---

[21] Two Wolves - A Cherokee Parable - Prepare For Change

Chapter 9

THE KING OF TYRE

One prevalent doctrine taught in the church is that Satan was next in line to the throne and fell because of pride. Some theologizers teach that Satan was 2nd in command and his name was Lucifer. Multiple passages taken from the Book Isaiah chapter 14 have been interpreted incorrectly and incorporated into the Body of Messiah as doctrines:

> How you have fallen from heaven, O star of the morning, son of the dawn! You have been cut down to the earth, You who have weakened the nations!
>
> –Isaiah 14:12, NASB

Lucifer in fourth-century Latin was a name for Venus, the morning star. It is derived from a term meaning "bright light." *Encyclopedia Britannica* states:

> Lucifer, (Latin: Lightbearer) Greek Phosphorus, or Eosphoros, in classical mythology, the morning star (i.e., the planet Venus at dawn); personified as a male figure bearing a torch, Lucifer had almost no legend, but in

poetry he was often herald of the dawn.

Isaiah 14 in its original Hebrew context contains no hint to a being named Lucifer. How did a Latin word get into a Hebrew text? Scholars hired by the King James court to translate the Bible into current English did not use the original Hebrew texts, but rather, they used various translations such as Saint Jerome's from the 4th century. This Latin word *Lucifer* soon transmuted into a disobedient angel cast out of heaven. The context of Isaiah is not about a fallen angel but about King Nebuchadnezzar. The Hebrew text reads, *"ech nafalta meshamim helel ben shachar"*: "How art thou fallen from heaven, bright shining one, son of the morning!" Jerome's translation reads, "How are you fallen from heaven, O Lucifer, son of the morning?" According to James B. Prichard, *Ancient Near Eastern Text*, in Belshazzar's day, every city throughout Mesopotamia had a ruling planet or constellation. The planet Venus, the bright shining star of the morning, *(Brown Driver Briggs Hebrew English Lexicon* no. 1966) was the ruling planet over the city of Babylon where Belshazzar was king.

Hebrew scholar, author and teacher Dr. Skip Moen expounds on this in his blog titled *The Lucifer Myth*:

> One translation found in Jerome has caused much difficulty and misunderstanding, namely, his translation of Isaiah 14:12. This is the first time that this word, Lucifer, appears in the biblical text. Jerome's use of the

word Lucifer has led to the development in Christian circles to the concept of Lucifer as the embodiment of the evil one, i.e., Satan or the Devil. The question now becomes where did Jerome get the idea of translating *helel ben shachar or heosphoros* to Lucifer when the passage is a specific reference to the planet Venus and Babylon? The answer is that Jerome did not strictly translate the Hebrew *helel ben shachar*, nor does it appear that he translated the Greek LXX heosphoros. It seems rather that he translated as though the original Greek word had been *lukophos*, meaning morning twilight. By following the trail of Greek etymology, we see that *luekeios* is an epithet for Apollo and Pan. The word *Lukay* not only means morning twilight but is an epithet for the Greek gods Apollo and Pan and also means the god of light. (Liddell and Scott Page 1064.) [22]

To reiterate, Lucifer does not exist in the Hebrew text nor the Greek translation, the Septuagint. It came from Jerome's 4th century A.D. translation of this verse into Latin. Lucifer is a Latin name that never existed in a Hebrew/Greek manuscript written before Latin even existed. The prophet Isaiah was burdened by Babylon. "The burden of Babylon, which Isaiah the son of Amos did see" (Isaiah 13:1, KJV):

---

[22] https://skipmoen.com/2018/01/the-lucifer-myth/

On the day the Father gives you relief from your suffering and turmoil and from the harsh labor forced on you, you will take up this taunt against the King of Babylon: How the oppressor has come to an end!

–Isaiah 14:4, KJV

When Isaiah proclaimed that a man had fallen from heaven, he was referring to the King of Babylon, Nebuchadnezzar. In Isaiah 14:13, the King is said to have shouted with great pomp that he would exalt his throne above God. Now, the King of Babylon is cut down. "For you have said in your heart: 'I will ascend into heaven, I will exalt my throne above the stars of God; I will also sit on the mount of the congregation On the farthest sides of the north" (Isaiah 14:13, NKJ). The King said, "I will sit also upon the mount of the congregation--the word rendered "congregation" is *moed* which means to fix, appoint. These refer to the appointed times—the Holy One's feasts days listed in Leviticus 23. The Holy One has had enough. The King is falling from his throne, and Tyre will no longer flourish.

Satan was not a cherub perfect in beauty. The Holy One was speaking to a very prideful location and people none other than Tyre:

The word of the LORD came to me again, saying, "Now you, son of man, take up a dirge {funeral poem to be sung} for Tyre, and say to Tyre, who lives at the entrance to the sea, merchant of the peoples to many coastlands, 'Thus says the Lord GOD, "O Tyre, you have said, 'I am perfect in beauty.'"

–Ezekiel 27:1-3, AMP

This lamentation is addressed to Tyre, concerning its favorable situation for trade. Tyre was sitting on two harbors gaining wealth. King Hiram, Nebuchadnezzar's stepfather, and ruler of Tyre, began to imagine that he was a god instead of being grateful to God for allowing him to live to a ripe old age and amongst such luxuries.

Also, the prophet Ezekiel mentions many earthly kings in poetic prose. They, too, are listed as being in the Garden of Eden. This language leads the reader back to the fall of Adam in the garden, figuratively. Most theologians base their doctrines concerning Satan on two passages from the prophets. The first passage is taken from Ezekiel:

> You were the signet of perfection, full of wisdom and perfect in beauty. You were in Eden, the garden of God; every precious stone was your covering, sardius, topaz, and diamond, beryl, onyx, and jasper, sapphire, emerald, and carbuncle; and crafted in gold were your settings and your engravings. On the day that you were created they were prepared. You were an anointed guardian cherub.
>
> –Ezekiel 28:12-14, ESV

Gathering more information brings clarity to whom the prophet was speaking about in these verses. In Ezekiel Chapter 1, Ezekiel gives chronological dates and the name of the king at the time of his writings:

> Now it came to pass in the thirtieth year, in the fourth month, in the fifth day of the month, as I was among the captives by the river of Chebar, that the heavens were opened, and I saw visions of God. In the fifth day of the month, which was the fifth year of king Jehoiachin's captivity.
>
> –Ezekiel 1:1-3, NASB

The date of this captivity is thought to be around 597 B.C. Further verified again when we read the same story in II Kings:

> At that time the servants of Nebuchadnezzar king of Babylon came up to Jerusalem, and the city was besieged. And Nebuchadnezzar king of Babylon came to the city while his servants were besieging it, and Jehoiachin the king of Judah gave himself up to the king of Babylon, himself and his mother and his servants and his officials and his palace officials.
>
> –II Kings 24:10-12, ESB

Further, the Prophet Ezekiel wrote in length about the conditions of Adonai's people and what was going to happen to them, similar to Jeremiah's warnings. Ezekiel also gives us much detail about the character of the men in charge during that time period, and with careful attention, the reader is able to unveil what most likely is the true identity of this "cherub that covered."

> In the eleventh month of the twelfth year, on the first day of the month, the word of the LORD came to me, saying, "Son of man, because Tyre has said of Jerusalem, 'Aha! The gate to the nations is broken; it has swung open to me; now that she lies in ruins I will be filled,' therefore this is what the Lord GOD says: 'Behold, O Tyre, I am against you, and I will raise up many nations against you, as the sea brings up its waves.'"

> –Ezekiel 26:1-3, BSB

How could Tyre be Satan when it's a city with a fleshly man who reigns over it? Is it a metaphor and an allegory that depicts a double meaning? The king over this busy port called Tyre received word that Nebuchadnezzar had burned the city of Jerusalem and that their gates were broken down. In his arrogance, the king of Tyre boasts over how he can prosper due to their weakened condition:

> "Aha, now I will prosper even more!" The word of the Lord came to me: "Son of man, say to the Prince of Tyre, Thus says the Lord God: "Because your heart is proud, and you have said, 'I am a god, I sit in the seat of the gods, in the heart of the seas,' yet you are but a man, and no god, though you make your heart like the heart of a god."

> –Ezekiel 28:1-2, NASB

Ezekiel goes on to discuss the wisdom this king had and all the wealth it brought him. The passage from Ezekiel 28 says this Prince is but a "man." It does not say this king is a fallen angel with superpowers. It says, "You are but a man!"

Continuing in Ezekiel 28:

> Ezekiel, son of man, tell the king of Tyre that I am saying: You are so arrogant that you think you're a god and that the city of Tyre is your throne. You may claim to be a god, though you're nothing but a mere human. You think you're wiser than Daniel and know everything. Your wisdom has certainly made you rich, because you have storehouses filled with gold and silver. You're a clever businessman and are extremely wealthy, but your wealth has led to arrogance!
>
> –Ezekiel 28:3-5, CEV

Does Satan have treasuries? Does an angel need gold or silver? Does Satan sit in the heart of the seas? This king had made much wealth. How?

> By your great wisdom in your trade you have increased your wealth, and your heart has become proud in your wealth.
>
> –Ezekiel 28:3-5, ESV

The city of Tyre was a place of considerable trade and bustle: much gold and silver and costly items. Tyre looked on Jerusalem and its gates that had fallen and had no compassion but immediately thought about making more wealth. Tyre was a

Phoenician city with one of the most active seaports for sailors and merchants of the world. It was indeed the principal profit-making seaport in the whole Eastern Mediterranean. *Amazing Bible Timeline with World History* has much information to glean concerning this city:

> The city of Tyre had a vast seaport. This seaport is what allowed the city to have a monopoly on the coastal trade routes that existed in the Mesopotamian region. Tyre's routes began in the east near modern day Lebanon and extended all the way to the west near modern day Spain. Many famous ancient cultures such as Egyptians, Romans and Greeks conducted business with the Phoenicians. Tyre also had sent colonists to the tip of North Africa in the west and established a powerful city-state known as Carthage. [23]

In Ezekiel 28, Adonai was speaking through his prophet Ezekiel and explaining what was going to happen to Tyre as a result of the king's pride. The king of Tyre was affiliated with David and his son Solomon. The money he made from Solomon alone would have been astronomical in that time:

> And Hiram King of Tyre sent messengers to David, and cedar trees, also carpenters and masons who built David a house. And David knew that the Lord had established

---

[23] Tyre Principal Seaport of Phoenicia – Amazing Bible Timeline with World History

him king over Israel and that he had exalted his kingdom for the sake of his people Israel.

–II Samuel 5:11, NASB

In addition, the king of Tyre is involved in the construction of David's house. He supplied David with cedar, carpenters, and even masons. Israel would have used its own tradesmen and suppliers if it were available to them. Further, King Hiram of Tyre supplied Solomon with the means to build a House for Adonai. This information is important because it reveals the temple language often mistaken for "the cherub that covers." Adam, God's chosen king/priest, was called to cultivate the Garden of Eden, but he and his wife broke the covenant and were banished. Now, similarly this king of Tyre will be banished and fall from his position of authority as well. *Delitzsch Biblical Commentary on the Old Testament* adds another layer to the comparison:

> Ezekiel here compares the situation of the prince of Tyre with that of the first man in Paradise; and then, in Ezekiel 28:15 and Ezekiel 28:16, draws a comparison between his fall and the fall of Adam. As the first man was placed in the garden of God, in Eden, so also was the prince of Tyre placed in the midst of paradisiacal glory. [24]

---

[24] https://biblehub.com/commentaries/ezekiel/28-14.htm

King Hiram of Tyre is referred to as an anointed cherub ordained for his position of authority. Now the roaring prophet Ezekiel proclaims he is falling from heaven metaphorically since he considered himself a god:

> Now Hiram King of Tyre sent his servants to Solomon when he heard that they had anointed him king in place of his father, for Hiram always loved David. And Solomon sent word to Hiram, "You know that David my father could not build a house for the name of the Father his God because of the warfare with which his enemies surrounded him until the Lord put them under the soles of his feet. But now the Lord my God has given me rest on every side. There is neither adversary nor misfortune. And so I intend to build a house for the name of the Lord my God, as the Lord said to David my father, 'Your son, whom I will set on your throne in your place, shall build the house for my name. Now therefore command that cedars of Lebanon be cut for me. And my servants will join your servants, and I will pay you for your servants such wages as you set, for you know that there is no one among us who knows how to cut timber like the Sidonians."
>
> –Kings 5:1-6, ESV

Tyre and Sidon were roughly 20 miles apart--very close in proximity. Tyre is the Phoenician city often mentioned together with Sidon. (Joshua 10:29). Tyre still exists today.

The Book of Ezekiel prophesies the destruction of this city called Tyre in chronological order:

> The word of the Lord came to me: "Son of man, take up a lament concerning the king of Tyre and say to him: 'This is what the Sovereign Lord says: You were the seal of perfection full of wisdom and perfect in beauty. You were in Eden, the garden of God; every precious stone adorned you: carnelian, chrysolite and emerald, topaz, onyx and jasper, lapis lazuli, turquoise and beryl. Your settings and mountings were made of gold; on the day you were created they were prepared. You were anointed as a guardian cherub, for so I ordained you."
>
> —Ezekiel 28:11-14

Also, note that cherubs which covered the ark were golden angels hand crafted by men, which covered the Ark of the Covenant. The king of Tyre supplied the building materials for these items and also for the temple built by Solomon. "For the cherubim spread their wings over the place of the ark, so that the cherubim made a covering over the ark and its poles" (II Chronicles 5:8 NASB).

The passage from Ezekiel 28 says that the person was in Eden, the garden of God. This passage is talking about the king of Tyre. In the Book of Ezekiel, Ezekiel is talking about other people said to have been in Eden, and all of them are fleshly men. By the time we reach Ezekiel 31, the prophet leaves off discussing Tyre and moves on to Egypt and Pharaoh. Pharaoh also was said to be prideful and stationed in the Garden of Eden:

> In the eleventh year, in the third month, on the first day of the month, the word of the LORD came to me: "Son of man, say to Pharaoh king of Egypt and to his multitude: 'Whom are you like in your greatness? Behold, Assyria was a cedar in Lebanon, with beautiful branches and forest shade, and of towering height, its top among the clouds.'"

–Ezekiel 31:1-3, ESV

The passages are written in poetic prose concerning trees, with comparisons to nations and rulers, then by verses 8- 9, one tree is described as greater, more beautiful and envied:

> The cedars in the garden of God could not rival it, nor the fir trees equal its boughs; neither were the plane trees like its branches; no tree in the garden of God was its equal in beauty. I made it beautiful in the mass of its branches, and all the trees of Eden envied it, that were in the garden of God.

–Ezekiel 31:8-9, ESV

Who is this tree that all the other trees envied? By the end of chapter 31, the reader plainly knows:

> Whom are you thus like in glory and in greatness among the trees of Eden? You shall be brought down with the trees of Eden to the world below. You shall lie among the

uncircumcised, with those who are slain by the sword. This is Pharaoh and all his multitude, declares the Lord God.

–Ezekiel 31:18, ESV

In this allegorical writing style, Pharaoh was in Eden, as well as the King of Tyre. Of course, neither was there. For example, seven candlesticks represent seven churches, but the candles are not literal churches. They are a comparison, allegorical.

Continuing in Ezekiel 28:

You were in Eden, the garden of God. Every precious stone was your covering: The ruby, the topaz and the diamond; The beryl, the onyx and the jasper; The lapis lazuli, the turquoise and the emerald; And the gold, the workmanship of your settings and sockets, Was in you. On the day that you were created they were prepared.

–Ezekiel 28:13, NASB

Many have affiliated these precious stones in Ezekiel 28 with the priestly garments and the breast plate featuring the 12 stones depicting the 12 tribes of Israel. However, further study provides even more information. In Ezekiel 26, a subtitle heading in most translations says, "Judgement on Tyre". In chapter 27, a subtitle reads "Lament over Tyre."

Looking deeper, Ezekiel chapter 28 explains all the jewels mentioned. The city of Tyre was bustling with trade. Picture the gold rush in California. The jewels are all mentioned as commerce and as stones hidden in the soil in the chapter. Adonai was speaking through Ezekiel, stating that the city of Tyre was adorned with precious stones. How? One way was the merchants bringing them. That's how they paid for cedar trees and labor. Remember, the scripture says, "Every precious stone adorned you or was your covering" (Ezekiel 28:13, ESV):

> The men of Dedan traded with you Tyre. Many coastlands were your own special markets; they brought you in payment ivory tusks and ebony.

> –Ezekiel 27:15, ESV

> Syria did business with you because of your abundant goods; they exchanged for your wares emeralds, purple, embroidered work, fine linen, coral, and ruby.

> –Ezekiel 27:16, ESV

The purple dye the Hebrews used on the priestly robes was made from a mollusk or snail from Tyre. This red dye, also known as Tyrian purple, was one of the most important commodities they exchanged. Tyre was so economically powerful at that time that the city's fame had spread all over the world. Of course, every stone adorned King Hiram as costly stones were placed on the robes and crowns of kings:

> The traders of Sheba and Raamah traded with you; they exchanged for your wares the best of all kinds of spices

and all precious stones and gold.

–Ezekiel 27:22, ESV

The prophet Ezekiel describes the king of Tyre and this seaport in much the same way as he describes Pharaoh, King of Egypt, in chapter 31.

Therefore, how do we know that "the cherub that covers" is not Satan? When reading Ezekiel 28 in its entirety, the main topic and person is King Hiram. Also, Adonai had Moses make two golden cherubs with outstretched wings to guard the Ark of the Covenant. We also know that Tyre had more than likely supplied or even crafted the cherubs Solomon had erected in the Temple. The King of Tyre provided the entire construction and the men to build it.

Newer translations such as the NET say:

> I placed you there with an anointed guardian cherub; you were on the holy mountain of God; you walked about amidst fiery stones.

–Ezekiel 28:14, NET

The guardian cherubs were assigned to keep sinful Adam and Eve out of the Garden, and their images also guarded the Ark of the Covenant. These angelic beings are guardians of God's purposes for righteousness. In the King James translation, Tyre was located on the holy mountain of God. In fact, Tyre is twelve miles north of the Israeli border. This king of Tyre swelled up at the mention of the destruction that happened in Jerusalem. He did not care if it were Adonai's holy people. He was going to take even more advantage of the situation. The king of Tyre was anointed as king, but like Adam, he had failed to stand for righteousness.

Both Pharaoh and the king of Tyre were said to be in Eden. There is no written record of any fallen angel in the Torah. According to the Torah and writings, angels are without sin. The word *angel* is a Hebrew word for messenger, and it can mean a spirit being or a human. Ancient Hebrew scholar, Jeff Benner explains more concerning this:

> Looking at where English translators have retained the word angel (111x) in the Old Testament from the Greek translation, the Hebrew word is #4397 מַלְאָךְ măl'âk, mal-awk'; from an unused root meaning to dispatch as a deputy; a messenger; specifically, of [Elohim], i.e. an angel (also a prophet, priest or teacher). The words used in the Old Testament to translate this Hebrew word are messenger (98x), ambassadors (4x) and kings (1x). The phrase the angel of Yahweh using the Greek word angel or the măl'âk of Yahweh using the Hebrew word măl'âk, simply means the messenger of Yahweh, the ambassador of Yahweh or the representative of Yahweh which is used in relation to both non-human beings in the invisible spirit world and to human beings in the visible physical

world. According to *Strong's Exhaustive Concordance of the Bible*, both the Greek word angel and the Hebrew word măl'âk are also applicable to a pastor, a prophet, a priest or a teacher. Even to physical ruling heads of governments and countries on earth. [25]

A few examples of how this word *angel* has been used in scripture:

This is he of whom it is written, "Behold, I send my messenger before thy face, who shall prepare thy way before thee."

–Matthew 11:10, RSV

Behold, I send my messenger to prepare the way before me.

–Malachi 3:1, RSV

In Malachi 3:1, the Hebrew word translated as messenger is מלאך (*mal-akh*, Strong's #4397), in the New Testament, this word is translated as *angel* and as *messenger*. When the Hebrew word *mal'lakh*, or the Greek word *aggelos*, is used, they refer to human messengers (even when the translators choose to use the word *angel*). A classic example of this can be found in Genesis:

Jacob went on his way and the angels (*mal'lakh*) of God met him; and when Jacob saw them he said, "This is God's

---

[25] https://www.ancient-hebrew.org/god-yhwh/some-do-not-believe-hes-an-angel.htm

army!" So he called the name of that place Mahanaim. And Jacob sent messengers *(mal'lakh)* before him to Esau his brother in the land of Seir, the country of Edom.

–Genesis 32:1-3, RSV

Clearly, multiple doctrines concerning fallen angels, cherubs, and an angel named Satan or Lucifer are due to translational errors, chapters, and books not read in their entirety. Well-meaning men have often preached with great authority about things they never had authority, or a good grasp of. Many of the doctrines concerning Satan are like the quote mentioned in an earlier chapter. "If you tell a big enough lie and tell it frequently enough, it will be believed." The Cherub mentioned in Ezekiel 28 was none other than a ruler over a territory likened to Eden or Paradise. In symbolic language, Ezekiel compares the situation of the King of Tyre with that of the first man in Paradise--the fall of Adam. And further, if God is all-knowing, without end or beginning, a Creator who brilliantly created the heavens and the earth and the fullness thereof, from the tiniest cell to the largest land and sea creatures, could this Creator of DNA make a mistake and create angelic beings like those who men such as Joshua fell on their faces in the presence of, with the capability to usurp the kingdom or fall from their position of power? The following chapter, *Can Angels Sin?* will cover this fascinating topic.

Chapter 10

CAN ANGELS SIN?

Can angel's sin? The most prevalent doctrine taught in Christianity is that angels fell into sin and slept with the daughters of men or the seed of Cain, and this caused giants to appear on the earth, but giants appeared after the flood as well. The passage used to teach this doctrine is found in Genesis 6:

> And it came to pass, when men began to multiply on the face of the earth, and daughters were born unto them, that the sons of God saw the daughters of men that they were fair; and they took them wives of all which they chose.
>
> –Genesis 6:1-2, KJV

Countless ministers teach that Satan was an angel who fell due to pride and that one-third of the angels left with him, but is this truth? II Peter 2 discusses angels chained in darkness in Tartarus. In Greek mythology, the Titans were people of massive proportions who were the offspring of Olympian gods. It was believed that the Titans were imprisoned in a section of the underworld called Tartarus:

> For if God did not spare the angels who sinned, but cast them down to hell (Tartarus) and delivered them into chains of darkness, to be reserved for judgment.
>
> —II Peter 2:4, NKJV

> And the angels who did not keep their position of authority but abandoned their proper dwelling—these he has kept in darkness, bound with everlasting chains for judgment on the great Day.
>
> —Jude 1:5-6, KJV

In the previous chapter, the word *angel* was highlighted as a word that often referred to a minister, a human messenger, a leader such as a prophet, priest, or servant as well as a spiritual being. Looking at II Peter 2:4, along with Jude 1:5-6, the word rendered *angels* is a matter of translational errors. A passage from the Book of Numbers helps solve this riddle concerning the underworld and Tartarus. It was Korah and 250 men who did not keep their positions of authority, but instead tried to usurp Moses and Aaron:

> Moses also said to Korah, "Now listen, you Levites! Isn't it enough for you that the God of Israel has separated you from the rest of the Israelite community and brought you near himself to do the work at the Lord's Tabernacle and to stand before the community and minister to them? He

has brought you and all your fellow Levites near himself, but now you are trying to get the priesthood too."

–Numbers 16:8-10, KJV

Also, in II Peter 2:4, Adonai Is talking about the wicked men in Noah's day, the wicked men of Sodom and Gomorrah, and also these men who followed Korah. They did not keep their positions of authority because they wanted to usurp the priesthood. They ended up chained in darkness underneath the earth. There is no other Biblical narrative of the earth swallowing men:

> Then Moses said, "This is how you will know that the Lord has sent me to do all these things and that it was not my idea: If these men die a natural death and suffer the fate of all mankind, then the Lord has not sent me. But if the Lord brings about something totally new, and the earth opens its mouth and swallows them, with everything that belongs to them, and they go down alive into the realm of the dead, then you will know that these men have treated the Lord with contempt."
>
> –Numbers 16:28-29, KJV

> As he finished speaking all these words, the ground that was under them split open; and the earth opened its mouth and swallowed them up, and their households, all the men who belonged to Korah with *their* possessions. So they and all that belonged to them went down alive to Sheol; and the earth closed over them, and they perished

from the midst of the assembly. All Israel who *were* around them fled at their outcry, for they said, "The earth may swallow us up!" Fire also came forth from the LORD and consumed the two hundred and fifty men who were offering the incense.

–Numbers 16:31-35, NASB

When we connect all of this information together from Jude and II Peter and the timeline of Moses and Korah, we see even further that the whole topic is unified. Continuing with the Book of Jude, we see more clues:

In the very same way, on the strength of their dreams, these ungodly people pollute their own bodies, reject authority and heap abuse on celestial beings. But even the archangel Michael, when he was disputing with the devil about the body of Moses, did not himself dare to condemn him for slander but said, "The Lord rebuke you!" Yet these people slander whatever they do not understand, and the very things they do understand by instinct—as irrational animals do—will destroy them.

–Jude 1:8-10, KJV

The Book of Jude, concerning a dispute over the Body of Moses, refers to the whole House of Israel. The devil mentioned is Korah. Moses was their leader. This is not referring to Moses's physical body. We read later that the Holy One buried Moses's physical body:

128

> So Moses the servant of the Lord died there in the land of Moab, according to the word of the Lord. And He buried him in a valley in the land of Moab, opposite Beth Peor; but no one knows his grave to this day.
>
> −Deuteronomy 34:5-6, NKJ

However, the Holy One also buried the people Moses had led through the wilderness. We call an assembly a Church Body. Moses' Body was the Children of Israel until Joshua took over:

> These were numbered by Moses and Eleazar the *kohen* when they counted *Bnei-Yisrael* on the plains of Moab across from Jericho. Not one of them was among those counted by Moses and Aaron the *kohen* when they counted *Bnei-Yisrael* in the Sinai wilderness, because *Adonai* had said they would surely die in the wilderness.
>
> −Numbers 26:63-65, TLV

Following Jude 1:8, we read that even the archangel Michael, when he was disputing with the devil (Korah) about the Body of Moses (Israel), did not dare to condemn him for slander but said, "The Lord rebuke you!" In Numbers 16, Moses confronts Korah and the usurpers and expresses how the Father has given them positions of authority, but now they are seeking the priesthood, too. Moses tells them they are banding together against *Adonai*! One of the most fascinating books on Satan was written by Duncan Heaster, *The Real Devil*. Heaster, a tutor at Aletheia

Bible College quickly ties in the Book of Enoch to II Peter and Jude 8, to bring straightforward comprehension and give the reader more clarity of Peters pleas concerning those who slander angelic beings by falsely stating that they slept with women:

> In the Book of Enoch, it is claimed that the righteous Angel Michael brings accusation against the 200 supposedly rebellious Angels, but Peter consciously contradicts this by stressing that "angels do *not* bring slanderous accusations against such beings in the presence of the Lord" (II Pet. 2:11), and Jude is even more specific by saying that this is true of Michael the Archangel (Jude 9). According to the Book of Enoch, the man Enoch judges the sinful Angels, but II Peter 3 warns that actually Angels will come with the Lord Jesus (Messiah Yeshua) in order to judge *men*. We can now understand why Peter claims that "bold and arrogant these men (the false teachers) are not afraid to slander celestial beings" (II Pet. 2:10)- i.e. the Angels. The Book of Enoch slandered Angels by claiming 200 of them sinned. As Jude 8 puts it, the false teachers "reject authority and slander celestial beings." The idea that the 200 Angels had sexual encounters with enticing women was therefore a slander. We need to reflect on the implications of all this- for claiming that Angels sin is actually spoken of by Peter and Jude as if it is serious blasphemy. Those early Christians were returning to their earlier Jewish and

Pagan beliefs, which according to II Pet. 2:22 is to be seen as a dog returning to its vomit. This is how serious the issue is. [26]

The Book of Jude informs us that these people slander whatever they do not understand. These men of Korah rejected Adonai's mighty prophet Moses' authority and Aaron's, and the earth swallowed them up. *Hell* is a word that has multiple meanings, and in this particular case, it means Tartarus from the Greek word *Tartaroo*, which is used only once in the Newer Testament in II Peter 2:4. This use of the word *hell* is not referring to a place of flaming fire. Angelic celestial beings cannot be chained. They disappear. They fly. The passages from Jude and II Peter describe Korah and the men who rose up against Aaron and Moses. In the Older Testament (*Tanakh*) the word *mal'ak*, was often translated *angel. Mal'ak* is used for human prophets in II Chronicles 36:15-16, Haggai 1:13; and Malachi 3:1. The "angels of the seven churches" in Revelation are human leaders as John would not be writing to a spirit angel.

"But even if we, or an angel from heaven, should preach to you a gospel contrary to what we have preached to you, he is to be accursed!" (Galatians 1:8 NASB). Again, *angel* is also a word for a prophet or a messenger of Adonai. Remember, John the Baptist was Adonai's chosen messenger, but according to this verse, others could have preached another gospel. Other angels?

---

[26] Jude and the Book of Enoch (realdevil.info)

No, other men. Can you imagine an angel standing in all its glory, able to soar and fly, appear, and disappear, said to do all Adonai's bidding, teaching a contrary gospel? Never:

> His created ones, who do His commands and obey Him. "Bless the LORD, O you his angels, you mighty ones who do his word, obeying the voice of his word!"
>
> –Psalm 103:20, NASB

He also has angels He sends to wreak havoc and destroy, but one thing is certain, He controls them. Destroying angels can also represent locust, flies, hail, and the plagues of Egypt:

> He sent upon them His burning anger, Fury and indignation, and trouble, A band of destroying angels.
>
> –Psalm 78:49, NASB

Regardless of what they are, they are His servants:

> And to which of the angels has he ever said, "Sit at my right hand until I make your enemies a footstool for your feet"? Are they not all ministering spirits sent out to serve for the sake of those who are to inherit salvation?
>
> –Hebrews 1:13-14, NASB

In Matthew 25, Yeshua Messiah corrects the Jewish sect of the Sadducees and used angels as a reference that confirms ignorance concerning angelic beings which was prevalent in 1st century Judaism as well:

The same day Sadducees came to him, who say that there is no resurrection, and they asked him a question, saying, "Teacher, Moses said, 'If a man dies having no children, his brother must marry the widow and raise up offspring for his brother.' Now there were seven brothers among us. The first married and died, and having no offspring left his wife to his brother. So too the second and third, down to the seventh. After them all, the woman died. In the resurrection, therefore, of the seven, whose wife will she be? For they all had her."

But Jesus answered them, "You are wrong, because you know neither the Scriptures nor the power of God. For in the resurrection they neither marry nor are given in marriage, but are like angels in heaven.

–Matthew 25:23-30, ESV

Below is a blog excerpt from Yahweh's Restoration Ministry, *The Sons of Elohim:*

The theory that angels mated with mortal women later crept into the Septuagint version. Of the three oldest manuscripts of the Septuagint, only the Codex Alexandrinus of the fifth century offers the word "angels" in Genesis 6:2 instead of "sons of Elohim." Not one of the Hebrew manuscripts, however, has the word "angels" in Genesis 6:2. Instead, all Hebrew manuscripts read "sons of

Elohim. [27]

The Book of Jasher, which is referred to in Joshua 10:13 and II Samuel 1:18, leads to more unveiling of this puzzle concerning fallen angels. According to Jasher it was not men sleeping with angels but wicked judges and rulers that went to the daughters of men and took their wives by force from their husbands according to their choice:

> There are at least three books published in modern times which have been called "The Book of Jasher," which are entirely different books. One is a Hebrew treatise on ethics, for which no one makes the claim of being a lost book of scripture. Another is an easily detected fraud, published in 1751, which claims to have been translated into English by Flaccus Albinus Alcuinus. It is sometimes called Pseudo-Jasher to distinguish it from the third Book of Jasher, which is a legitimate Hebrew document. [28]

Below is one of the apocryphal *Books of Jasher*. There are as many as five separate works by this title, all composed much later than Biblical times. This particular one is a translation of a Hebrew book printed in 1613. *Sepir Ha Yasher*:

> When Titus destroyed Jerusalem in AD 70, an officer named Sidrus discovered a hidden library complete with a

---

[27] The Sons of Elohim - Yahweh's Restoration Ministry (yrm.org)
[28] https://www.johnpratt.com/items/docs/lds/meridian/2002/jasher.html

scholar hiding there. The officer had mercy on the man and took him and the books to his residence at what is now Seville, Spain, but was then called Hispalis, capital of the Roman province Hispalensis. The manuscript was donated to the Jewish college at Cordova, Spain, and after printing was invented, the Jewish scholars had the book printed in Hebrew in Venice in 1625. [29]

Continuing in Jasher 4 verses 16, 17, and part of 18:

And all the sons of men departed from the ways of the Lord in those days as they multiplied upon the face of the earth with sons and daughters, and they taught one another their evil practices and they continued sinning against the Lord. And every man made himself a god, and they robbed and plundered every man his neighbor as well as his relative, and they corrupted the earth, and the earth was filled with violence. And their Judges and Rulers went to the daughters of men and took their wives by force from their husbands according to their choice.

–Jasher 4:16-18

This type of wickedness is illustrated in our century by ISIS, the cartel, and other evil and corruptions that have fallen on earth. Angelic beings were created perfect and were never put out of heaven. Scripture implies that angelic beings are perfect and

---

[29] https://www.johnpratt.com/items/docs/lds/meridian/2002/jasher.html

created for Adonai:

> Praise Him, all His angels; Praise Him, all His hosts! Praise Him, sun and moon; Praise Him, all stars of light! Praise Him, highest heavens, And the waters that are above the heavens! Let them praise the name of the LORD, For He commanded and they were created. He has also established them forever and ever; He has made a decree which will not pass away.
>
> −Psalm 148:2-6, NASB

When reading scriptures concerning messengers or angelic beings, we must look at the whole passage and the story's context to define whether it refers to a human or an angel. Jasher confirms that men in places of authority had become so corrupt that they were consumed with their fleshly desires, and any woman they saw that was beautiful, married, or single, they took as their own.

In Psalm 148, we learned that angelic beings were created perfectly. Satan is not an angel. Lucifer is a Latin word that crept into a Hebrew text in error. The dragon many say is Satan is described in Revelation:

> Then another sign appeared in heaven: and behold, a great red dragon having seven heads and ten horns, and on his heads were seven diadems. And his tail swept away a third of the stars of heaven and threw them to the earth. And the dragon stood before the woman who was about to give

birth, so that when she gave birth he might devour her child.

–Revelation 12:3-4, NASB

Is Satan a dragon, and do the stars accurately represent fallen angels in Revelation 12? Does Satan have seven heads, ten horns, and seven crowns on his head? Or are these symbolic, a metaphor, for kingdoms and rulers of kingdoms. It is kings who wear crowns, not angels. The passage from Revelation 12 describes the worldly kings of the earth. Yeshua told the people:

> Why do you not understand what I am saying? Is it because you cannot hear my words? "You are of your father the devil, and you want to do the desires of your father."

–John 8:43-44, NASB

These leaders standing before the Messiah were not fallen angels whose father was the devil. This is figurative language. This passage represents men who could not hear the Word of Adonai. Their father wasn't literally Satan. They had earthly fathers. Their fathers were the religious leaders who had brainwashed them. Author and teacher Joel Huan Sects explains the issues during Yeshua's day highlighting the two sects among the Parasitical schools and their leaders in his article "During Biblical Times — Pharisees:"

Among the Pharisees were two schools of thought, based

on the teachings of two rabbis, Shammai and Hillel. Shammai called for a strict, unbending interpretation of the Law on almost every issue, but Hillel taught a looser, more liberal application. Followers of Shammai fostered a hatred for anything Roman, including taxation—Jews who served as tax collectors were persona non grata. The Shammaites wanted to outlaw all communication and commerce between Jews and Gentiles. The Hillelites took a more gracious approach and opposed such extreme exclusiveness. Eventually, the two schools within Pharisaism grew so hostile to each other that they refused to worship together. [30]

The strict school of Shammai is where the term "synagogue of Satan," originated. Those who sat under Shammai's leadership were told their father was the devil (an adversary). They did not want Yeshua to be King. They were in control, and they loved the power, wealth, and control of the people (Anti-Christ).

When they came to arrest Yeshua and Peter drew his sword, Yeshua told him this: "Or do you think that I cannot appeal to My Father, and He will at once put at My disposal more than twelve legions of angels?" (Matthew 26:23, NASB). Twelve legions are more than 36,000 angels. He doesn't seem concerned about any fallen ones or about these men who have come to

---

[30] https://wulfstein.org/2020/11/20/sects-during-biblical-times-pharisees-a/

arrest him. Yeshua called men who were using the Torah as a weapon, evil serpents:

> You serpents, you brood of vipers, how are you to escape being sentenced to hell? Therefore I send you prophets and wise men and scribes, some of whom you will kill and crucify, and some you will flog in your synagogues and persecute from town to town, so that on you may come all the righteous blood shed on earth, from the blood of righteous Abel to the blood of Zechariah the son of Barachiah, whom you murdered between the sanctuary and the altar. Truly, I say to you, all these things will come upon this generation.
>
> –Matthew 23:33-36, ESV

These men were not factually snakes. This Babylonian system will be hurled down at the end of days. This system that has destroyed and taken from the poor, the widows, and the orphans, and has piled up for itself kingdoms on earth with money it has stolen from the needy, will one day be judged.

When studying serpents and snakes, we must look at the heavens. The beast in Revelation 13 has seven heads, and the constellation Draco is the Greek word for dragon and is referred to as the serpent, dragon, and devil. It has a tail, and it sweeps the stars and causes meteor showers. In an article by Kim Ann Zimmermann *Draco Constellation: Facts about the Dragon*, *Draco* is defined as a Latin term meaning serpent:

Despite its size and designation as the eighth-largest constellation, Draco, the "dragon" constellation, is not especially prominent. The name is derived from the Latin term draconem, meaning "huge serpent," and the constellation literally snakes its way through the northern sky. The head of the dragon consists of four stars (Beta, Gamma, Nu and Xi Draconis) in a trapezoid and located just north of Hercules. From there, the dragon's body winds its way through the sky, ending between the Big Dipper and Little Dipper. From early to mid-October, a meteor shower known as the Draconids appears to radiate from Draco's head. [31]

Returning to Revelation 12:1-5:

A great sign appeared in heaven: a woman (Virgo/Rachel/ Israel) clothed with the sun (Father), with the moon (Celestial calendar/Feast/His seasons) under her feet, and a crown of twelve stars (Twelve Tribes) on her head. She was pregnant and cried out in pain as she was about to give birth. Then another sign appeared in heaven: an enormous red dragon (Constellation Draco/ adversary/ Babylonian System) with seven heads and ten horns and seven crowns on its heads. Its tail swept a third of the stars out of the sky and flung them to the earth. The dragon stood in front of the woman who was about to give birth so that it might

---

[31] https://www.space.com/16755-draco-constellation.html

devour her child the moment he was born. She gave birth to a son, a male child (Exodus 4:22: Israel-My firstborn son), who "will rule all the nations with an iron scepter." And her child was snatched up to God and to his throne.

The woman (Israel) fled into the wilderness to a place prepared for her by God, where she might be taken care of for 1,260 days (3.5 years or 1st half of tribulation):

> Now he had still another dream, and related it to his brothers, and said, "Lo, I have had still another dream; and behold, the sun (Rachel) and the moon (Jacob) and eleven stars (Eleven brothers plus Joseph, all twelve tribes) were bowing down to me.
>
> –Genesis 37:9, NASB

What is happening in the heavens is playing out on the earth. "On earth as it is in Heaven" might have a deeper meaning than we thought. We look to the moon for the Holy One's calendar and Festivals:

> The heavens are telling of the glory of God; And their expanse is declaring the work of His hands. Day to day pours forth speech, and night to night reveals knowledge. There is no speech, nor are there words; Their voice is not heard. Their line has gone out through all the earth, and their utterances to the end of the world. In

them, He has placed a tent for the sun, which is as a bridegroom coming out of his chamber; it rejoices as a strong man to run his course.

–Psalm 19:1-5, NASB

The Holy One has placed His clock in the sky for times, seasons, and yes, prophecy. In conclusion to our intellectual question, angels do not sin, nor do they have sexual relations with humans and procreate:

Yeshua answered and said unto them, ye do err, not knowing the scriptures, nor the power of God. For in the resurrection, they neither marry, nor are given in marriage, but are as the Angels of God in heaven.

–Matthew 22:29, KJV

Chapter 11

SATAN IN THE NEW TESTAMENT

Below is a list of verses with Satan in the New Testament. Each verse has been summarized in its original context as to what or who Satan represents in each passage given. Due to multiple telling's of the temptation of Messiah in the gospels, I have left the bulk of commentary concerning this event at the end:

1. Then saith Jesus unto him, Get thee hence, Satan: for it is written, Thou shalt worship the Lord thy God, and him only shalt thou serve.

    –Matthew 4:10, KJV

2. And if Satan cast out Satan, he is divided against himself; how shall then his kingdom stand?

    –Matthew 12:26, KJV

3. But he turned, and said unto Peter, Get thee behind me, Satan: thou art an offence unto me: for thou savourest not the things that be of God, but those that be of men.

    –Matthew 16:23, KJV

4. And he was there in the wilderness forty days, tempted of Satan; and was with the wild beasts; and the angels ministered unto him.

–Mark 1:13, KJV

5. And if Satan rise up against himself, and be divided, he cannot stand, but hath an end.

–Mark 3:26, KJV

6. And these are they by the wayside, where the word is sown; but when they have heard, Satan cometh immediately, and taketh away the word that was sown in their hearts.

–Mark 4:15, KJV

7. But when he had turned about and looked on his disciples, he rebuked Peter, saying, Get thee behind me, Satan: for thou savourest not the things that be of God, but the things that be of men.

–Mark 8:33, KJV

8. And Jesus answered and said unto him, Get thee behind me, Satan: for it is written, Thou shalt worship the Lord thy God, and him only shalt thou serve.

–Luke 4:8, KJV

9. And he said unto them, I beheld Satan as lightning fall from heaven. Behold, I give unto you power to tread on

serpents and scorpions, and over all the power of the enemy: and nothing shall by any means hurt you.

–Luke 10:18, KJV

10. If Satan also be divided against himself, how shall his kingdom stand? because ye say that I cast out devils through Beelzebub.

–Luke 11:18, KJV

The Messiah was tested in all points just as we are, and He overcame in the wilderness:

For we do not have a high priest who is unable to sympathize with our weaknesses, but one who in every respect has been tempted as we are, yet without sin.

–Hebrews 4:15, ESV

Our Messiah was a carpenter and a teacher with a mother and father. He had siblings. He has a culture and ethnicity, and he gets angry. He weeps. Although Yeshua was the Son of the Holy One, we are told in Hebrews 5 that he learned obedience from the things which He suffered. Each reference to Yeshua in the Gospels showcases his humanity. Hebrews chapter 5 makes this clear. The Messiah wept, and he suffered:

In the days of his flesh, Jesus offered up prayers and supplications, with loud cries and tears, to him who was able to save him from death, and he was heard because of his reverence. Although he was a son, he learned obedience through what he suffered.

–Hebrews 5:7-8, ESV

The adversary, or Satan, Yeshua is battling, is his own nature. Yeshua learned obedience through suffering. Does the Holy One need to learn obedience? Yeshua was sweating drops of blood, and many times he was emotional because he had all the emotions and desires of any other human. Although Yeshua was empowered from High, the verses clarify that he was also a man. We also know he was tempted and suffered while being tempted:

Since, therefore the children share in flesh and blood, he himself likewise partook of the same things, that through death he might destroy the one who has the power of death, that is, the devil, and deliver all those who through fear of death were subject to lifelong slavery. For surely it is not angels that he helps, but he helps the offspring of Abraham. Therefore he had to be made like his brothers in every respect, so that he might become a merciful and faithful high priest in the service of God, to make propitiation for the sins of the people. For because he himself has suffered when tempted, he is able to help those who are being tempted.

–Hebrews 2:14-18, ESV

Moving forward and as we continue through the portions from the New Testament, look at each verse with a different lens:

11. And ought not this woman, being a daughter of Abraham, whom Satan hath bound, lo, these eighteen years, be loosed from this bond on the sabbath day?

–Luke 13:16, KJV

This passage may be about the woman's infirmities, but on a deeper level, the woman was bent over from the heavy loads the Pharisees had placed upon her and the people. Yeshua points out that they would loose or free their animal but not this woman who had been under their bondage for 18 years. In Hebrew, the word for life, *chai (chet, yohd)*, is also the number eighteen. This woman needed to walk upright but had been bound because of certain Pharisees from the Beit of Shammai and their harshness. However, Yeshua was Torah observant, and He kept many of the traditions. To repeat as discussed in chapter 9, also discussed on p. 102, there were two primary schools or sects of Pharisees in power at the time of Yeshua who opposed one another. The *Beit* (house/school) of Shammai and the *Beit* (house/school) of Hillel. These schools had one main difference, The House of Shammai was anti-non-Jew and did not want to accept them into the fold and teach them Torah or the commandments of the Holy One. On the other hand, Hillel was compassionate and wanted to bring them into the fold and teach them wisdom and understanding so they could be a light to the nations.

Torah and Temple Investigation, a Messianic website, explains the woman in bondage and the number 18 in their blog *The Synagogue of Satan – Just Who is Yeshua Railing Against?*

> When Shammai gained his power, Hillel became the deputy Nasi, meaning he had to submit to Shammai. Shammai then passed what are known in the Talmud as 'The 18 Edicts of Shammai." These edicts were designed to separate Jews from Non-Jews as Shammai was vehemently anti-Non-Jew. It is these 18 edicts that form the basis for what we read about in the Apostolic Writings concerning Peter and his vision of the sheet or the middle wall of separation Paul talks about. It was HaShem telling Peter and Paul these 18 edicts of Shammai are NOT of Him, and He is telling them both to disregard them. Even the Talmud Bavli in tractate Shabbat 17a says when these 18 edicts were issued, "And that day was as difficult for Israel as the day the Golden Calf was made." These 18 edicts were a disaster for Israel and are the main cause of the disputes between Yeshua and the Pharisees. The point is, Yeshua was railing against the SHAMMAI PHARISEES and not all the Pharisees as Christendom teaches, for He Himself was a Pharisee of Beit Hillel just as Paul was a Pharisee of Beit Hillel. This doesn't mean Hillel was perfect--by no means, and it doesn't mean Yeshua didn't

take issue with some of his rulings either, but for the most part, Yeshua sided with Hillel. It is said that 'The School of Shammai binds and the School of Hillel loosens." [32]

With this information, we can read the passage in Luke with more understanding:

> Now he was teaching in one of the synagogues on the Sabbath. And behold, there was a woman who had had a disabling spirit for eighteen years. She was bent over and could not fully straighten herself. When Jesus saw her, he called her over and said to her, "Woman, you are freed from your disability." And he laid his hands on her, and immediately she was made straight, and she glorified God. But the ruler of the synagogue, indignant because Jesus had healed on the Sabbath, said to the people, "There are six days in which work ought to be done. Come on those days and be healed, and not on the Sabbath day." Then the Lord answered him, "You hypocrites! Does not each of you on the Sabbath untie his ox or his donkey from the manger and lead it away to water it? And ought not this woman, a daughter of Abraham whom Satan bound for eighteen years, be loosed from this bond on the Sabbath day?" As he said these things, all his adversaries were put to shame, and all the people rejoiced at all the

---

[32] https://torahandtempleinvestigations.com/2021/05/28/the-synagogue-of-Satan-just-who-is-yeshua-railing-against/

glorious things that were done by him.

–Luke 13: 10-17, ESV

12. "Then entered Satan into Judas surnamed Iscariot, being of the number of the twelve" (Luke 22:3, KJV). Again, going deeper, can Satan enter us? Remember when Peter spoke against Yeshua suffering on the cross and Yeshua answered him in this manner:

> But he turned and said to Peter, "Get behind me, Satan! You are a hindrance to me. For you are not setting your mind on the things of God, but on the things of man."

–Matthew 16:23, ESV

In both cases, Judas and Peter were an adversary. Their minds were not on the things of the Holy One. Judas let his mind and money become a Satan to himself. Peter could not see that death and resurrection were the Father's plan for His Son. He spoke as an adversary because he did not understand what must occur:

13. And the Lord said, Simon, Simon, behold, Satan hath desired to have you, that he may sift you as wheat: But I have prayed for thee, that thy faith fail not: and when thou art converted, strengthen thy brethren.

–Luke 22:31, KJV

Peter, in this moment, has a problem Esau had. Peter's flesh nature is his worst adversary. Yeshua informs Peter that he will be converted. This transformation happens after significant testing and his denial of Messiah Yeshua:

> 14. And after the sop Satan entered into him. Then said Jesus unto him, That thou doest, do quickly.
>
> –John 13:27, KJV

Judas' behavior at the Seder did not exhibit any typical characteristics of what many would call possession (Luke 22:3). He is not growling or foaming or crying out. There is no evidence to show that Satan had taken control of his physical body. What we read shows that Judas had become an instrument used to betray the Messiah and Yeshua knows this. Judas had succumbed to the voice of temptation and, in essence, opened the door for the adversary to control his actions. This is similar to what we see concerning Cain:

> The LORD said to Cain, "Why are you angry, and why has your face fallen? If you do well, will you not be accepted? And if you do not do well, sin is crouching at the door. Its desire is contrary to you, but you must rule over it.
>
> –Genesis 4:3, ESV

> 15. But Peter said, Ananias, why hath Satan filled thine heart to lie to the Holy Ghost, and to keep back part of the price of the land?
>
> –Acts 5:3, KJV

Both passages above (Gen. 4:3, Acts 5:3) mimic Judas's behavior. In both stories, men became filled with their own evil desires of their flesh. Judas walked with the Messiah for over three years. Something happened that allowed him to choose to stray from the path of righteousness. The wages of sin is death, but the gift of God is true life through the Messiah. Judas was sowing into his flesh nature until Satan had entered him. He became his own adversary by the choices he made:

> 16. To open their eyes, and to turn them from darkness to light, and from the power of Satan unto God, that they may receive forgiveness of sins, and inheritance among them which are sanctified by faith that is in me.
>
> —Acts 26:18, KJV

What does it mean to turn from the power of Satan, and what would that have meant in that time period? The Apostle Paul is speaking before King Agrippa, and he is quoting from a passage found in Isaiah the prophet:

> I am the LORD; I have called you in righteousness; I will take you by the hand and keep you; I will give you as a covenant for the people, a light for the nations, to open the eyes that are blind, to bring out the prisoners from the dungeon, from the prison those who sit in darkness. I am the LORD; that is my name; my glory I give to no other, nor my praise to carved idols.
>
> —Isaiah 42:6-8, ESV

The power of Satan (adversary) is the idolatry of the world and the things of the word, not a fallen angel:

> 17. And the God of peace shall bruise Satan under your feet shortly. The grace of our Lord Jesus Christ be with you. Amen.
>
> –Romans 16:20, KJV

Notice the passage says "Shortly" or "soon" in other translations. Paul, in and around 57 A.D when the Book of Roman's was written, was hopeful Satan or the adversaries of the world would be crushed soon. Today, we can clearly see that much is going on concerning adversaries. Many government leaders are corrupt. The murder rate keeps skyrocketing. Racial tensions, poverty, sex trafficking, and drugs are prevalent in our society. Pushing agendas concerning gender, vaccines, and a "woke" generation have become common language. Men in positions of power like Pharaoh bring much corruption and bondage. The translation from Roman's 16 in *The Scriptures* version reads as follows: "And the Elohim of peace shall crush Satan under your feet shortly. The favour of our Master יהושע Messiah be with you. Amĕn" (Romans 16:20, ISR). The apostle Paul felt sure that Yeshua was returning to set up His Kingdom shortly, but it has been over 2,000 years since these words were written. The Kingdom of heaven is at hand. Messiah in us is the hope of glory. We shine light and make disciples bearing fruit and doing the works of the kingdom:

18. To deliver such an one unto Satan for the destruction of the flesh, that the spirit may be saved in the day of the Lord Jesus.

–I Corinthians 5:5, KJV

How does one deliver people in their assembly over to Satan? One cannot knock on the devil's door and say, "Excuse me, Satan, I have a person for you." In this letter, Paul is dealing with many issues at Corinth. Corinth had a variety of religions, such as its Greek and Roman gods and goddesses. But Paul is correcting a man for sleeping with his father's wife. Later, after Paul's harsh correction, he leads with compassion and yearns to bring the person who had been "turned over to Satan" back into the community and treat him with love, knowing that we all sin and need forgiveness. Reading the passage fully explains why Paul would use such language more precisely. By removing a person caught in adultery from the assembly, the person now has plenty of time to think about what he has done wrong, such as Miriam, Moses's sister who was placed outside the camp, away from the fellowship, for seven days for gossip and slander concerning Moses's wife. Paul is using the same technique. Following is the passage fully:

It is actually reported that there is sexual immorality among you, and of a kind that is not tolerated even among pagans, for a man has his father's wife. And you are arrogant! Ought you not rather to mourn? Let him who

156

has done this be removed from among you. For though absent in body, I am present in spirit; and as if present, I have already pronounced judgment on the one who did such a thing. When you are assembled in the name of the Lord Jesus and my spirit is present, with the power of our Lord Jesus, you are to deliver this man to Satan for the destruction of the flesh, so that his spirit may be saved in the day of the Lord.

–I Corinthians 5:1-5, ESV

Moving to II Corinthians, we read Paul explaining more concerning this man who was handed over to Satan:

For such a one, this punishment by the majority is enough, so you should rather turn to forgive and comfort him, or he may be overwhelmed by excessive sorrow. So I beg you to reaffirm your love for him.

–II Corinthians 2:7-8, ESV

19. Do not deprive one another, except perhaps by agreement for a limited time, that you may devote yourselves to prayer; but then come together again, so that Satan may not tempt you because of your lack of self-control.

–I Corinthians 7:5, ESV

This passage concerns those who refrain from sexual relations inside a marriage. Paul clarifies that this is fine during a short season of prayer and fasting if both parties agree. The reference to Satan (adversary) here is, again, our own evil tendencies. The lust of the eye and the desires of our flesh. Satan has never walked into a store and bought a porn magazine. Satan is not forcing a person's eyeballs to look at someone lustfully. Satan did not force a television evangelist to pick up prostitutes. It was his flesh nature. Like you and I and every other human, we battle an adversary:

> 20. Lest Satan should get an advantage of us: for we are not ignorant of his devices.
>
> —II Corinthians 2:11, KJV

Again, this passage from I Corinthians 5:5 concerns the man caught in adultery who Paul declares must be removed and handed over to Satan for the destruction of the flesh. Afterward, Paul says to bring him back into the assembly lovingly:

> But if anyone has caused grief, he has not grieved me, but all of you to some extent—not to be too severe. This punishment which was inflicted by the majority is sufficient for such a man, so that, on the contrary, you ought rather to forgive and comfort him, lest perhaps such a one be swallowed up with too much sorrow. Therefore I urge you to reaffirm your love to him. For to this end, I also wrote, that I might put you to the test, whether you are obedient in all things. Now whom you forgive

anything, I also forgive. For if indeed I have forgiven anything, I have forgiven that one for your sakes in the presence of Christ, lest Satan should take advantage of us; for we are not ignorant of his devices.

–II Corinthians 2:5-11, NKJ

21. And no marvel; for Satan himself is transformed into an angel of light.

–II Corinthians 11:14, KJV

Paul wanted the assembly in Corinth to realize that although he removed the person, it was now time to bring him back into the community so that he could be ministered to. If left alone and without the strength of the gospel being preached and people to hold him accountable, he might fall back into sins, Satan's devices, or the lust of the flesh.

Paul has written extensively in II Corinthians about false prophets and "super" apostles and those who have tried to come in and distort the Gospel and bring a false Messiah. Before delving into the main point Paul made in II Corinthians 11:14, where he states, "And no wonder! For Satan himself transforms himself into an angel of light," we must gather information as to whom this statement is directed:

For if someone comes and proclaims another Jesus than the one we proclaimed, or if you receive a different spirit

159

from the one you received, or if you accept a different gospel from the one you accepted, you put up with it readily enough. Indeed, I consider that I am not in the least inferior to these super-apostles. Even if I am unskilled in speaking, I am not so in knowledge; indeed, in every way we have made this plain to you in all things.

–II Corinthians 11:4-6, ESV

After speaking and using sarcasm, Paul explains these men and their character by explaining that they appear to be shepherds and use boasting to entice the younger ones. The verses prior explain the context:

And what I am doing I will continue to do, in order to undermine the claim of those who would like to claim that in their boasted mission they work on the same terms as we do. For such men are false apostles, deceitful workmen, disguising themselves as apostles of Christ. And no wonder, for even Satan disguises himself as an angel of light. So it is no surprise if his servants, also, disguise themselves as servants of righteousness.

–II Corinthians 11:12-15, ESV

Paul explains that these "false Apostles" are deceitful workmen and will be found out by their deeds. He says that the adversary disguises himself as a messenger of light. We are often enticed by something or someone in leadership that appears good and holy, but Paul says watch their deeds or lack thereof:

> 22. Wherefore we would have come unto you, even I Paul, once and again; but Satan hindered us.

> –I Thessalonians 2:18, KJV

The apostle Paul had plenty of enemies, and he was very vocal about several, including the false apostles, also referred to as super-apostles, not to mention the disputes the Jews and the Stoics and Epicurean philosophers had with him. These many enemies hindered Paul, not Satan. Dr. Skip Moen explains more concerning who Satan represents to a first-century audience in his Hebrew word study *Essenes, Rabbis, and Christians:*

> The problem with Satan is that the Tanakh never really treat ha-Satan as a uniquely identifiable being. In the Tanakh, ha-Satan is more like an office in the heavenly court, an adversary whose job is to raise questions about human loyalty and obedience. In fact, the word is used for real human persons, not just divine figures. But by the time Hellenism had penetrated the thinking of the Mediterranean world, all of this changed. In the Qumran documents, "The angel of darkness is the same as Belial elsewhere, whom God has created, with whom he is in conflict, who oppresses the righteous, and who will finally be judged. The term *Satan* occurs in the Scrolls only three times in obscure connections."

Moen continues, in later Judaism, "The rabbis suggest that the devil is a fallen angel, although Qumran finds no place for this view." In the Gospels, Satan has a role much like the accuser in Job (an office). It's worth noting: "In general, the NT does not refer to a primal fall of Satan." [33]

23. Even him, whose coming is after the working of Satan with all power and signs and lying wonders.

–II Thessalonians 2:9, KJV

Studying this verse concerning Satan, we must look at the whole chapter and its context:

> The coming of the lawless one will be accompanied by the working of Satan, with every kind of power, sign, and false wonder, and with every wicked deception directed against those who are perishing, because they refused the love of the truth that would have saved them. For this reason God will send them a powerful delusion so that they believe the lie, in order that judgment may come upon all who have disbelieved the truth and delighted in wickedness.

–II Thessalonians 2:9-12, BSB

This passage concerns lawlessness, which means *Torahlessness*. The coming of the lawless one has been very prevalent in our day.

---

[33] https://skipmoen.com/2019/06/essenes-rabbis-and-christians/

The working of the adversary is just what it is, and we see a watered-down gospel that is powerless. We see wolves in sheep's clothing and false prophets doing false signs and wonder. At the beginning of II Thessalonians 2, Paul discusses the man of lawlessness. In verse 8, he says, "And then the lawless one will be revealed, whom the Lord Jesus will slay with the breath of His mouth and annihilate by the majesty of His arrival" (II Thessalonians 2:8, BSB). This lawless "one" is not one man but "man" in general. Yeshua is the Word made flesh, and by His Words, he will slay the lawless one with fire that purifies:

> 24. Of whom is Hymenaeus and Alexander; whom I have delivered unto Satan that they may learn not to blaspheme.
>
> –I Timothy 1:20, KJV

In I Timothy 2, we learn the details of what Hymenaeus was doing that was causing false doctrine and division:

> But avoid irreverent babble, for it will lead people into more and more ungodliness, and their talk will spread like gangrene. Among them are Hymenaeus and Philetus, who have swerved from the truth, saying that the resurrection has already happened. They are upsetting the faith of some.
>
> –I Timothy 2:16-18, ESV

The Apostle Paul is giving the same formula he presented in I Corinthians 5:5, concerning the man who had slept with his father's wife. Compare number **#18** on this list for more on "turning one over to Satan." As far as Alexander, in I Timothy 11:20, we read more concerning Alexander the coppersmith and his title in II Timothy 4; however, the name Alexander occurs 6 times in the Newer Testament and describes up to five different men:

> Alexander the coppersmith did me great harm; the Lord will repay him according to his deeds. Beware of him yourself, for he strongly opposed our message. At my first defense no one came to stand by me, but all deserted me. May it not be charged against them!
>
> –II Timothy 4:14, ESV

Again, Alexander the coppersmith could be the man mentioned in II Timothy, but we do not know if he is the same man mentioned in I Timothy. Paul encountered many Greeks who resisted his preaching because it harmed their businesses. Demetrius was a silversmith in Ephesus who made the silver shrines of Artemis. One of these men named Alexander was blasphemous and had not learned maturity or humility. Paul warned Timothy. In prison, Paul expresses how Alexander and Demetrius have damaged the gospel of Yeshua by their slander and pride:

25. For some are already turned aside after Satan.

–I Timothy 5:15, KJV

The passage from I Timothy 5:15 refers to women and the trouble that often comes with idle women who spend much time gossiping or slandering others. When Paul warns Timothy, he lets him know that some of these women in the assembly have already turned aside to their evil inclination and are not walking in Messiah:

> But refuse to enroll younger widows, for when their passions draw them away from Christ, they desire to marry and so incur condemnation for having abandoned their former faith. Besides that, they learn to be idlers, going about from house to house, and not only idlers, but also gossips and busybodies, saying what they should not. So I would have younger widows marry, bear children, manage their households, and give the adversary no occasion for slander. For some have already strayed after Satan.
>
> –I Timothy 5:11-15, ESV

> 26. I know thy works, and tribulation, and poverty, (but thou art rich) and I know the blasphemy of them which say they are Jews, and are not, but are the synagogue of Satan.
>
> –Revelation 2:9, KJV

Similar language is found in the Dead Sea Scrolls, where a small persecuted Jewish sect considered the rest of Judaism apostate and called its persecutors "the lot of Belial" (Satan). During the time of the Messiah, there were two schools among the Pharisees. Shammai and Hillel were the chief rabbis over these schools. Gamaliel, Paul's teacher, was the grandson of Hillel. These two schools had drastically different views. Shammai drove off perspective proselytes, whereas Hillel accepted them graciously. When Paul began drawing the Gentiles into the Kingdom and teaching and preaching the good news, this caused great fear among the strict Jews connected to the leadership. Shammai was frank and stern. According to him, Gentiles had no part in the World to Come. However, Hillel was more accepting.

Hope of Israel ministry in the heart of Jerusalem, whose main aim is to bring the hope of the Messiah back to Israel, has an in-depth article on these two schools of thought titled *The Pharisees, Hasidim, and the Early Judahite Ecclesia*, in which the author further describes the school of Shammai and their intolerance of making disciples by not allowing those who were not Jews to learn the Torah:

> According to the Talmud, Shammai's temporary success in forcing his views through on a number of issues, and thus humiliating Hillel, was a day of sorrow and lamentation in Israel -- "that day was as grievous for Israel as the day on which they made the Golden Calf." According to modern Rabbinic scholars, that generation of Pharisees -- because of the power of the school of

166

Shammai, undoubtedly -- was "an unworthy generation." Interestingly, Yeshua the Messiah himself said much the same thing. Yeshua declared: "An evil and an adulterous generation seeketh after a sign" (Matthew 12:39). Speaking of cities where he had done mighty miracles, Yeshua said, "It shall be more tolerable for the land of Sodom in the day of judgment than for thee" (Matthew 11:21-24). Of course, the wickedness of the Sadducees and Herod the king and his coterie of sycophants and boot-lickers also made that generation a truly unworthy and wicked one.

A certain gentile once came to Hillel and said, "I'm ready to become a Jew, but only if you can teach me the whole Torah while I stand on one foot." Hillel replied, "What is hateful to you, don't do to your fellow man; that is the whole Torah, and the rest is just commentary. Go then and learn it" (Shabbat 31a; p. 95 of *The Life and Teachings of Hillel*). [34]

The school of Shammai was referred to as the synagogue (School) of Satan (an adversary) due to his harshness and strict intolerance of those who were not Jews. Hopefully, this brings enlightenment to the passage from Revelation:

---

[34] https://www.hope-of-israel.org/hasidim.htm

27. I know thy works, and where thou dwellest, even where
    Satan's seat is: and thou holdest fast my name, and hast
    not denied my faith, even in those days wherein Antipas
    was my faithful martyr, who was slain among you, where
    Satan dwelleth

–Revelation 2:13, KJV

In Revelation 2, we learn of a man named Antipas. History states
that Antipas was sentenced to death on the Altar of Zeus inside a
brazen bull. This contraption was one of the evilest inventions of
all time:

> According to Diodorus Siculus, in 560BC, Perilaus, a
> metalsmith from Athens, designed the brazen bull.
> Perilaus made the contraption for the Phalaris, the despot
> of the Sicilian city of Acragas. Phalaris was known for his
> excessive cruelty, and so, with this in mind, Perilaus
> designed something especially unpleasant for Phalaris to
> execute his enemies in. As the name suggests, the brazen
> bull was a hollow metal vessel in the shape of a bull. The
> condemned were forced inside through a trapdoor in the
> bull's belly and then enclosed within. Once the victim was
> secured, a fire was lit beneath the bull, heating the metal-
> and cooking the unfortunate victim. Pipes fitted to the
> bull's mouth converted the sounds of the victim's
> agonized screams into: "the tenderest, most melodious,
> most pathetic of bellowing's," as Perilaus described them

168

when he was pitching the bull to Phalaris. [35]

Antipas was killed where Satan dwells. This unusual description is mentioned in several other places, and Pergamum is said to be where Satan's throne is:

> And to the angel of the church in Pergamum write: 'The words of him who has the sharp two-edged sword." 'I know where you dwell, where Satan's throne is. Yet you hold fast my name, and you did not deny my faith even in the days of Antipas my faithful witness, who was killed among you, where Satan dwells. But I have a few things against you: you have some there who hold the teaching of Balaam, who taught Balak to put a stumbling block before the sons of Israel, so that they might eat food sacrificed to idols and practice sexual immorality.
>
> —Revelation 2:12-14, ESV

The assembly or church in Smyrna and Philadelphia had some people from the synagogue of Satan, and the assembly in Thyatira went after the deep things of Satan. These passages refer more than likely to those from the school of Hillel and the harsher school of Shammai.

For more on these schools, see #26:

---

[35] 12 Torturous Methods of Execution in History that Will Make You Squirm (historycollection.com)

28. But unto you I say, and unto the rest in Thyatira, as many as have not this doctrine, and which have not known the depths of Satan, as they speak; I will put upon you none other burden.

–Revelation 2:24, KJV

Pergamum had several temples dedicated to the Roman Imperial cult. Pergamum was acquainted with many gods and many forms of entertainment. Dr. Eli Lizorkin-Eyzenberg, author and scholar at Israeli Institute of Biblical Studies, in her article *What Is the Throne of Satan,* uncovers the hidden meaning of this passage:

> Other than temples to emperors and even to the goddess Roma, the city held the high honor of hosting and maintaining a temple to Zeus – Father of all gods and man and the ruler of Olympians on Mt. Olympia in accordance with ancient Greek beliefs. Zeus was closely associated with the Roman deity Jupiter whose name means the sky or literally the "heavenly father" god. The altar to Zeus was one of the most impressive structures in Pergamum. The altar's stairs, columns, and sculptured sides once stood forty feet (12 meters) high. Today, only the steps around the altar's base can be seen in the Pergamum Museum in Berlin. The sides of the altar were ornamented with marble panels depicting a mythical battle between

Greek gods and rebellious giants who were the sons of Mother Earth.

Many have suggested that this altar to Zeus is what is meant by the throne of Satan in Revelation 2:13. But there exist a number of other possibilities – such as the Asclepius cult headquarters or a concentration of the Imperial and Roman cult in that city. In Roman antiquity, the image of a sword and especially a double-edged sword was highly symbolic. So, in this city, it can truly be said that it hosted the throne of Satan, the symbol of Roman Imperial authority and rule. Christ introduced himself to the assembly of the followers of Israel's God in Christ as "the one who has the sharp two-edged sword." If the above identification of the throne of Satan as a Roman imperial cult is correct, then it would make perfect sense for Christ here to be presented as someone with the authority of the double-edged sword. [36]

29. Behold, I will make them of the synagogue of Satan, which say they are Jews, and are not, but do lie; behold, I will make them to come and worship before thy feet, and to know that I have loved thee.

–Revelation 3:9, KJV

---

[36] What is the Throne of Satan? (israelbiblicalstudies.com)

See notes on #25-28 for an explanation concerning the school of Shammai referred to as the synagogue (School) of Satan (an adversary) due to his harshness and strict intolerance of those who were not Jews:

30. And the great dragon was cast out, that old serpent, called the Devil, and Satan, which deceiveth the whole world: he was cast out into the earth, and his angels were cast out with him.

–Revelation 12:9, KJV

There is no Hebrew word for "*devil.*" Judaism represents a pure monotheism which does not allow for any Power other than God. Monotheism is the belief in only one god that created the world who is omnipotent, omnipresent, omnibenevolent, and omniscient. Again, the Hebrew word *Satan* means to accuse, denounce, and bring charges against. In Judaism, ancient and modern, the Satan is a title, not a name. The passage in Revelation 12 mentions angels, which are representatives or messengers who work under this beastly system of the world. The word *angel* is a Hebrew word for messenger, and it can mean a spirit being or a human. In chapter 8, we learned from Hebrew scholar Jeff Benner that the Hebrew word for angel is #4397 מַלְאָךְ mǎl'âk, mal-awk'; from an unused root meaning to dispatch as a deputy; a messenger; specifically, of [Elohim], i.e., an angel (also a prophet, priest or teacher). According to *Strong's Exhaustive Concordance of the Bible*, both the Greek word angel and the Hebrew word mă l'âk are also applicable to a pastor, a prophet, a priest, or a teacher. Even to physical ruling heads of governments and countries on earth. [37]

The devil and Satan refer to kingdoms and dogmas that deceive the world, such as politicians and corrupt rulers, as well as false prophets and men in powerful religious domains. These rulers use their wealth and means to control world leaders and governments. Those who work under the beastly system are messengers or cohorts. Those deceived and following the harlot are warned to "come out of" this system:

> After this I saw another angel coming down from heaven, having great authority, and the earth was made bright with his glory. And he called out with a mighty voice, "Fallen, fallen is Babylon the great! She has become a dwelling place for demons, a haunt for every unclean spirit, a haunt for every unclean bird, a haunt for every unclean and detestable beast. For all nations have drunk the wine of the passion of her sexual immorality, and the kings of the earth have committed immorality with her, and the merchants of the earth have grown rich from the power of her luxurious living." Then I heard another voice from heaven saying, "Come out of her, my people, lest you take part in her sins, lest you share in her plagues; for her

---

[37] https://www.ancient-hebrew.org/god-yhwh/some-do-not-believe-hes-an-angel.htm

sins are heaped high as heaven, and God has remembered her iniquities. Pay her back as she herself has paid back others, and repay her double for her deeds; mix a double portion for her in the cup she mixed. As she glorified herself and lived in luxury, so give her a like measure of torment and mourning, since in her heart she says, 'I sit as a queen, I am no widow, and mourning I shall never see.' For this reason her plagues will come in a single day, death and mourning and famine, and she will be burned up with fire; for mighty is the Lord God who has judged her." And the kings of the earth, who committed sexual immorality and lived in luxury with her, will weep and wail over her when they see the smoke of her burning. They will stand far off, in fear of her torment, and say, "Alas! Alas! You great city, you mighty city, Babylon! For in a single hour your judgment has come." And the merchants of the earth weep and mourn for her, since no one buys their cargo anymore, cargo of gold, silver, jewels, pearls, fine linen, purple cloth, silk, scarlet cloth, all kinds of scented wood, all kinds of articles of ivory, all kinds of articles of costly wood, bronze, iron and marble, cinnamon, spice, incense, myrrh, frankincense, wine, oil, fine flour, wheat, cattle and sheep, horses and chariots, and slaves, that is, human souls. The fruit for which your soul longed has gone from you, and all your delicacies and your splendors are lost to you, never to be found again!"

The merchants of these wares, who gained wealth from her, will stand far off, in fear of her torment, weeping and mourning aloud, "Alas, alas, for the great city that was clothed in fine linen, in purple and scarlet, adorned with gold, with jewels, and with pearls! For in a single hour all this wealth has been laid waste." And all shipmasters and seafaring men, sailors and all whose trade is on the sea, stood far off and cried out as they saw the smoke of her burning, "What city was like the great city?" And they threw dust on their heads as they wept and mourned, crying out, "Alas, alas, for the great city where all who had ships at sea grew rich by her wealth! For in a single hour she has been laid waste. Rejoice over her, O heaven, and you saints and apostles and prophets, for God has given judgment for you against her!" Then a mighty angel took up a stone like a great millstone and threw it into the sea, saying, "So will Babylon the great city be thrown down with violence, and will be found no more; and the sound of harpists and musicians, of flute players and trumpeters, will be heard in you no more, and a craftsman of any craft will be found in you no more, and the sound of the mill will be heard in you no more, and the light of a lamp will shine in you no more, and the voice of bridegroom and bride will be heard in you no more, for your merchants were the great ones of the earth, and all nations were deceived by your sorcery. And in her was found the blood of prophets and of saints, and of all who have been slain on earth."

–Revelation 18, ESV

When we read the entire chapter, we learn that these are earthly kingdoms controlled by men like Pharaoh and the king of Tyre. These kingdoms are the same type of kingdoms very present in Moses's day and Yeshua's day. The blood of the prophets was found in her and the blood of saints:

31. And he laid hold on the dragon, that old serpent, which is the Devil, and Satan, and bound him a thousand years.

–Revelation 20:2, KJV

This 1000 years represents the wedding supper of the lamb. It is the longest Sabbath, a time of rest, and those who are following the true Messiah and have not been deceived will rule and reign with Him:

32. Blessed and holy is the one who shares in the first resurrection! Over such the second death has no power, but they will be priests of God and of Christ, and they will reign with him for a thousand years.

–Revelation 20:6, ESV

33. And when the thousand years are expired, Satan shall be loosed out of his prison.

–Revelation 20:7, KJV

After "the thousand years," the adversary will be loosed. This is the final count down. The Reign of Messiah Yeshua begins during the fall feasts, the feasts of trumpets. The Messiah will reign on earth with the saints and Israel for a thousand years. "Over such the second death has no power, but they will be priests of God and of Christ, and they will reign with him for a thousand years" (Revelation 20:6, ESV). A Millennial Reign is a future event referred to as Jacob's Trouble. The prophet Jeremiah speaks of such a day and time:

> These are the words that the LORD spoke concerning Israel and Judah: "Thus says the LORD: We have heard a cry of panic, of terror, and no peace. Ask now, and see, can a man bear a child? Why then do I see every man with his hands on his stomach like a woman in labor? Why has every face turned pale? Alas! That day is so great there is none like it; it is a time of distress for Jacob; yet he shall be saved out of it."
>
> –Jeremiah 30: 5-7, ESV

Yeshua Messiah will rule the earth from Jerusalem:

> Of the increase of his government and of peace there will be no end, on the throne of David and over his kingdom, to establish it and to uphold it with justice and with righteousness from this time forth and forevermore.
>
> –Isaiah 9:7, ESV

Just as Yahweh created the heavens and the earth in six days and then rested on the seventh, so, too, will man rest for the seventh. This is the longest Sabbath ever. Humans will strive with God for six Millennial days, and then the seventh will bring a Millennial day of rest. After the one-thousand-year reign, the adversary will be loosed. This is not a snake or a devil with horns or a fallen angel. This is wickedness. John calls governments and leaders' dragons, beasts, and other serpents. These are false beastly systems with men who rule over them. These systems will be hurled down and will not reign with power. When one is dead, they need resurrected, this, too, according to author and scholar James R Brayshaw, is a spiritual metaphor. He explains clearly in his book *Why Is Satan Loosed by God for 1000 Years in Revelation?*

> The destruction of the wicked is the second death, not eternal life in Hell. This state is metaphorically represented by the phrase, *"And the devil that deceived them was cast into the lake of fire and brimstone. . . "* A true "lake of fire" has never existed, and that is why John uses a metaphor as the place to cast in the personified sin and wickedness. The *"Dragon,"* *"Satan,"* the *"Devil,"* and that *"Old Serpent"* are all terms that represent the evil and wickedness that emanates from the heart of man. We must remember the heart is deceitfully wicked above all else. The deception that comes from our evil inclination

has long been called the "serpent" and certainly is old as we saw how Adam and Eve did not overcome it in the Garden. It is the resurrection of these wicked persons that is spoken of as the "loosing of Satan." This occurrence takes place so that the second resurrection, known to be those resurrected "to contempt," takes place, and then death has no more sting because when no one is alive who desires to do wickedly, then death is destroyed. This is important to remember because, according to the Scriptures, sin brings death. No more sin--no more death. From this point on, there will be no more death for anyone ever. Death was the last enemy and is now officially defeated. Paul speaks of this situation in this manner; "*I Corinthians 15:25-26, For he must reign, till he hath put all enemies under his feet. The last enemy that shall be destroyed is death.*" If you would like, you can stop reading right here as you see sense in saying that the binding of Satan is referring to wicked people who are dead during the Thousand Year Reign. In addition, the "loosing of Satan" is the resurrection of those wicked dead who want to become part of a Kingdom they rejected while they were alive. [38]

---

[38]

https://www.academia.edu/12004319/Why_Is_Satan_Loosed_By_God_for_1000_Years_in_Revelation

CLOSING

For a thousand years, Satan was scarcely mentioned in the writings spanning from the Book of Genesis to the last prophet Malachi of the Old Testament--a time span from 1446 BCE to 430 BCE What descriptions or beliefs would a 1st century Jewish audience have concerning the adversary? The information gathered in this book illustrates that Satan has been gaining ground and growing over time, but today more than ever. The false image of Satan needs to decrease, while Yeshua the Messiah needs to increase. What we focus on grows. Our adversary has no power unless the Holy One gives it to him.

This book has helped you reexamine and relook at the old serpent called the Devil and Satan with new eyesight. Some chapters may have been more difficult to digest than others. Still, each brings more examples of how the identity of this adversary may be hidden in some areas of scripture without diminishing the false dogmas that have crept in over time concerning Satan.

Why is it essential to get a better grasp on the true identity of the adversary? One reason, I believe, is that too often Satan gets blamed for everything and is given more power than he deserves. Unlearning the lies concerning the serpent helps us face our own evil inclination and battles of the flesh.

We looked at Ephesians 6:12, KJV, "For we wrestle not against flesh and blood, but against principalities, against powers, against the rulers of the darkness of this world, against spiritual wickedness in high places," and were able to identify these powers as the rulers in governments. We scrutinized the serpent who spoke in Genesis, along with the adversary who waged a bet with the Holy One that if Job were stripped of his prosperity and health, he would no longer serve Adonai as a humble servant. We inspected multiple passages in the Old Testament and New and weighed them for truth and original context.

We know that in Hebrew thought, Satan is the embodiment of evil. This pressure to sell one's birthright as Esau did for a bowl of red soup is inside us all. These desires to sin and be disobedient are a force within us, not an evil deity or an influence from without. The Apostle Paul makes this clearer:

> For the good that I wish to do, I do not do; but the evil I do not wish to do, this I practice. And if I do that which I do not wish, it is no longer I who work it, but the sin dwelling in me. I find therefore this law, that when I wish to do the good, that the evil is present with me. For I delight in the Torah of Elohim according to the inward man, but I see another law in my members, battling against the Torah of my mind, and bringing me into captivity to the law of sin which is in my members.

Wretched man that I am! Who shall deliver me from this body of death? Thanks to Elohim, through יהושע Messiah our Master! So then, with the mind I myself truly serve the Torah of Elohim, but with the flesh the law of sin.

–Romans 7:19-25, ISR

Indeed, there are two urges inside us, one to do evil and the other to do righteousness. A person's character is determined by which of the two impulses is dominant. The good impulse controls the righteous, and the evil impulse controls the wicked. Each of us battle these impulses just as Paul, Abraham, Isaac, Jacob, Esau, and every other human being, regardless of how esteemed we are in the world or our circles of influence. When Satan is placed in a seat of authority and made more powerful than he is, we can mistake our trials and tests as something happening to us by a mean Devil who will get his in the end instead of looking in a mirror or asking the Holy One why we are going through so much turmoil. Many times, it is because we are being pruned and prepared, as was Joseph, who was thrown into a pit, falsely accused, hated, and imprisoned. When faced with his brothers who wanted him dead, Joseph says, "But now, do not therefore be grieved or angry with yourselves because you sold me here; for God sent me before you to preserve life" (Genesis 45:5, NKJ). In the end, Joseph knew that the Holy One had allowed these things to happen. After Joseph was given a place of authority in prison, he was now almost ready to feed the world. Joseph learned how to deal with people who had been criminals and those who had been wrongfully accused. Joseph was placed on the Potter's Wheel for a season while the Holy One molded him into the exact person needed for the famine and to bring His people to one place and allow them to reproduce and become strong.

It was not Satan who was the cause of Joseph's rejection and trials. The Holy One is in control over all things even our conflicting impulses.

While *Satan Unmasked* examined the history and evolution of Satan, as well as examining the context of passages mentioning him, Book Two *Spirits Unveiled*, uncovers angelic hosts, demons, unclean spirits, and how they have evolved over time in contemporary writings and the entertainment industry.

The Book of Amos adds to the mystery: "If a trumpet is blown in a city, will not the people be afraid? If there is calamity in a city, will not the Lord have done it?" (Amos 3:6, NKJ). Throughout the Bible Adonai uses spirits as agents sent by Him and under His power, such as the incident in I Samuel: "But the Spirit of the LORD departed from Saul, and an evil spirit from the LORD troubled him" (I Samuel 16:14, KJV).

I hope you will join me in discovering more about the spirit world, angelic beings, demonic entities, possession, oppression, and deliverance by the power of the *Ruach HaKodesh* (Holy Spirit) in *Spirits Unveiled.*

Blessings,

Tekoa Manning

DON'T GO YET!

Thank you for reading Book I, *Satan Unmasked*, of the *Unmasking the Unseen Series*. I hope you continue with Book II, *Spirits Unveiled*, Book III, *Wolves Unseen*, and Book IV, *King Revealed*. These books have been a labor of love and have taken years of research to complete. Your feedback and thoughts are important to me.

COULD YOU HELP ME?

Please go to Amazon books and leave me an honest review. It would mean so much to me and help with our ministry to orphans in India and Malawi.

Please also refer this Book Series, *Unmasking the Unseen*, to those who may benefit from it. For updates and new book releases, go to Tekoamanning.com.

Blessings & Shalom,
Tekoa Manning
Manning the Gate Publishing LLC

Sources

1. Pelaia, Ariela, (2019) How Satan is Viewed in Judaism. Learn Religions. Retrieved 2-25-2020. https://www.learnreligions.com/jewish-view-of-Satan-2076775

2. Center for Global Christianity at Gordon-Conwell Theological Seminary, –pewforum.org. Retrieved on 7-12-2017. Status-of-Global-Christianity-2022.pdf (gordonconwell.edu)

3. Goebbels, Joseph. Inspiring Quotes. Retrieved 2-12-2022. https://www.inspiringquotes.us/quotes/TzEs_7CxEctuv

4. Woodbridge, Russell S. (6-4-2015) The Gospel Coalition--Prosperity Gospel Born in the USA. Retrieved 8-4-2021. https://www.thegospelcoalition.org/article/prosperity-gospel-born-in-the-usa

5. Wilkinson, Richard H. (2003) The Complete Gods and Goddesses of Ancient Egypt pp. 127–128. Retrieved on 4-8-2021. https://en.wikipedia.org/wiki/Osiris

6. Lane, Lonnie. (9-3-2009) Church Isn't In the New Testament. Retrieved 9-14-2014. https://sidroth.org/articles/church-isnt-new-testament

7. Bible Hub. Commentaries. (2004-2022). Leviticus 17:7. Retrieved on 10-02-2022. Keil and Delitzsch Biblical Commentary on the Old Testament. (2004 - 2021 by Bible Hub) Retrieved on 5-12-2020. https://biblehub.com/commentaries/leviticus/17-7.htm

8. Moen, Skip. (6-26-2019) Essenes, Rabbis, and Christians. Hebrew Word Study. Retrieved on 3-16-2020. https://skipmoen.com/2019/06/essenes-rabbis-and-christians

9. Hebrew Today. The Letter Mem. (no date). Retrieved on 10-4-2022. The Letter Mem (מ) - Hebrew Today

10. Abarim Publications (first published here on 2006-04-19; moved to present location on 2008-05-18) The Amazing Name Satan. Retrieved on 9-25-2022. satan | The amazing name satan: meaning and etymology (abarim-publications.com)

11. Abarim Publications (first published on 2008-05-18; last updated on 2022-05-13) The Amazing Name Kidron. Retrieved on 9-25-2022. Kidron | The amazing name Kidron: meaning and etymology (abarim-publications.com)

12. Wenk, Gary Ph.D. (7- 6-2021). Why Do Humans Keep Inventing Gods to Worship. Psychology Today. Retrieved on 9-27-2022. Why Do Humans Keep Inventing Gods to Worship? | Psychology Today

13. World Atlas. (No date given) Reasons Why Muslims Are The World's Fastest-Growing Religious Group. Retrieved on 9-27-2022. Reasons Why Muslims Are The World's Fastest-growing Religious Group - WorldAtlas

14. Messianic Jewish Alliance Of America. (2019) Messianic Movement. Retrieved on 9-28-2022. Messianic Movement | MJAA Messianic Jewish Alliance of America

15. Lohri, R. K. Boloji. (12-4-2005). Do Hindus Believe in More Gods than One? Retrieved on 9-28-2022. Do Hindus Believe in More Gods than One? by R. K. Lahri (boloji.com)

16. Buddho. The Editors. (No date). The 5 Precepts: Buddhism and Morality. Retrieved on 9-28-2022. The 5 Precepts: Buddhism and Morality | Buddho.org

17. Guthrie, Stan, Turning point. (3-18-2021). Ascending Mars Hill. Retrieved on 9-28-2022. Ascending Mars Hill - Breakpoint

18. Bible Hub. Strong's Lexicon. Acts 17:22. (no date) Retrieved on 10-01-2022. Acts 17:22 Parallel: Then Paul stood in the midst of Mars' hill, and said, Ye men of Athens, I perceive that in all things ye are too superstitious. (biblehub.com)

19. Best Greece Tours. (No date). SACRED MARS HILL (AREOPAGUS)! THE (1) ONE AND ONLY. Retrieved on 10-01-2022. Sacred Mars Hill (Areopagus)! The(1) one and only! (bestgreecetours.com)

20. Ferguson, Everett, Cult Prostitution in the New Testament: Journal of the Evangelical Theological Society 42.3 (1999): 443-460. Retrieved on 6-19-2019. https://biblicalstudies.org.uk/article_ephesus_baugh.html#

21. Guest Author. Two Wolves – A Cherokee Parable. (9-2-2021. Retrieved on 10-02-2022. Two Wolves - A Cherokee Parable - Prepare For Change

22. Moen, Skip, (1- 26-2018). The Lucifer Myth: Hebrew Word Study. Retrieved Retrieved on 1-14-2020. https://skipmoen.com/2018/01/the-lucifer-myth/

23. Hunter, Margaret. (5-24-2012) Amazing Bible Timeline with World History. Retrieved on 4-2-2022. Tyre Principal Seaport of Phoenicia – Amazing Bible Timeline with World History

24. Delitzsch Biblical Commentary on the Old Testament, (2004 - 2021 by Bible Hub) Retrieved on 6-12-2020. https://biblehub.com/commentaries/ezekiel/28-14.htm

25. Andrew, Augustus (August 2017) Ancient Hebrew, Some Do Not Believe He's an Angel. Retrieved on 10-12-2021. https://www.ancient-hebrew.org/god-yhwh/some-do-not-believe-hes-an-angel.htm

26. Heaster, Duncan. The Real Devil. The History of the Devil. (no date). Retrieved on 10-25-2022. Jude and the Book of Enoch (realdevil.info)

27. Yahweh's Restoration Ministry, The Sons of Elohim. (10-10-2016) Retrieved on 10-6-2020. The Sons of Elohim - Yahweh's Restoration Ministry (yrm.org)

28. Pratt, John, P. (Jan. 7, 2002) How Did the Book of Jasher Know? Reprinted from Meridian Magazine Retrieved on 8-12-2020. Book of Jasher (johnpratt.com)

29. Pratt, John, P. (Jan. 7, 2002) How Did the Book of Jasher Know? Reprinted from Meridian Magazine Retrieved on 8-12-2020. Book of Jasher (johnpratt.com)

30. Sects Huan Joel. (12-10-2020) During Biblical Times —
Pharisees. Retrieved on 2-13-2021.
https://wulfstein.org/2020/11/20/sects-during-biblical-
times-pharisees-a/

31. Zimmermann, Kim. (7-19-2017) Draco Constellation:
Facts About the Dragon, Draco. Retrieved on 5-1-2019.
https://www.space.com/16755-draco-constellation.html

32. Moshe, David. (5-28-2021) Torah and Temple
Investigation Ministry, The Synagogue of Satan – Just
Who is Yeshua Railing Against? Retrieved on 6-16-2021.
https://torahandtempleinvestigations.com/2021/05/28
/the-synagogue-of-Satan-just-who-is-yeshua-railing-
against/

33. Moen, Skip. (6-26-2019) Essenes, Rabbis, and
Christians. Hebrew Word Study. Retrieved on 3-16-
2020. https://skipmoen.com/2019/06/essenes-rabbis-
and-christians/

34. Hope of Israel ministry, The Pharisees, Hasidim, and the
Early Judahite Ecclesia. Retrieved on 2-20-2022
https://www.hope-of-israel.org/hasidim.htm

35. Sheldon, Natasha. (11- 15-2017) Ancient History
Blogsite. 12 Torturous Methods of Execution in History.
Retrieved on 3-13-2020 12 Torturous Methods of
Execution in History that Will Make You Squirm
(historycollection.com)

36. Lizorkin-Eyzenberg Eli, (5-2-2015) Israeli Institute of
Biblical Studies, What Is the Throne of Satan? Retrieved
on 6-13-2020 What is the Throne of Satan?
(israelbiblicalstudies.com)

37. Augustus, Paul, Andrew. Ancient Hebrew Research Center. (199-2022). Some Do Not Believe He's an Angel. Retrieved on 10-22-2022. Some Do Not Believe He's an Angel | AHRC (ancient-hebrew.org)

38. Brayshaw, James R, (Academia 2022) Chapter 23, page 157, Why is Satan Loosed by God for 1000 Years in Revelation? (PDF) Why Is Satan Loosed By God for 1000 Years in Revelations? | James R Brayshaw - Academia.edu

CPSIA information can be obtained
at www.ICGtesting.com
Printed in the USA
LVHW021132210523
747607LV00022B/479

9 781737 402022